GENEALOGY BITS AND BITES

A Collection of Newspaper Columns

By Marjorie Blocher Kinsey, CG

2000

MBK Publications

ISBN Number 0-615-11534-9

Copyright 2000 by

MBK Publications
1612 Southeast Blvd.
Evansville, Indiana 47714

Printed in the United States of America

TABLE OF CONTENTS

PREFACE

Tri-State Roots first appeared in the Evansville Sunday Courier and Press, Evansville, Indiana, on 13 October 1991, and has been published every other Sunday since. The focus of the column is to provide help to those who are interested in finding out more about their families. Material has also been presented that might interest and educate readers even though they may not now be actively doing genealogical research.

Queries have been included from time to time, as well as announcements about meetings, conferences and new publications of area genealogical and historical societies. All but the queries have been removed from this collection.

This collection represents most of what was published between October 1991 and January 1994. Some columns have not been included because the material was specific about an event which has come and gone, and some have been edited slightly. I hope this collection will help new readers as well as those who have forgotten about the first publication several years ago.

I wish to express thanks to the editorial staff of the Evansville Courier and Press for their willingness to take a chance with an untried writer. I believe they have been pleasantly surprised at the continued interest in genealogy and family history among their readers.

I wish to thank my husband, Philip Kinsey, for his continued help in making the computer and e-mail do what I want. I am only moderately literate in those languages and he helps the communication system go more smoothly.

The readers who write with questions and comments are a continuing inspiration. Without their steady encouragement I might have gone on to other projects instead. It's been a source of continuing education for me as I explore new subjects to include in *Tri-State Roots*. I hope this collection of columns will be useful to readers who are still looking for more ancestors.

Marjorie Blocher Kinsey
12 May 2000

CHAPTER 1

START AT THE BEGINNING

Start Search With Family Members

Q: You make it sound so easy to trace your ancestry. But when I checked the Mormon library computer about my great-grandfather, he wasn't there! What can I do that's easy?

A: There is an easy way to trace your ancestry: find someone else who has already begun to do it. If you find that several people have been working on the skeleton outline, you are especially lucky. You won't need to do every bit of the research yourself, but can specialize on individuals or events that interest you most.

However, if you seem to be the first in your family to wonder where the family came from you'll need to do some detective work. If you are just beginning, you must not skip any of the first steps in doing genealogical research.

I have read a dozen how-to books and they all have the same first chapter. The title reads something like "Start at Home and Start with Yourself".

Like every good detective, you must gather the facts that you already know. Search your memory for names and dates, starting with yourself and go from there to your parents, grandparents, aunts and uncles. Record your information on some kind of standardized form. Most how-to books have several samples that you can photocopy, and they will remind you of the facts you are looking for.

After you have exhausted your memory, look at things you have around your home. Newspaper clippings of marriages or deaths, funeral cards and old photos all can provide additional information you have forgotten. If you are just starting to research your family, you may not have any such articles so your next step will be to contact those relatives who are the paper savers. Your mother or uncle who has trouble throwing things away will be your salvation in adding to your family tree.

Ask them to start digging through their shoe boxes and envelopes for the papers they have saved. Check letters from other relatives. Did anyone leave a diary or a family Bible?

Along the way, quiz your parents or older relatives about their memories of family. Just because they don't talk about it does not mean they don't have some of the facts you seek.

Have any other relatives expressed interest in collecting family information? Don't reinvent the wheel; take advantage of the work that's already been done.

A whole new generation of ancestor hunters is emerging as many young people become curious about their family heritage. If you are among them, happy hunting. But I did not mean to mislead you into thinking it will always be easy. If you are the first in your family to look, it may be slow going, but everything you find will be exciting.

10 October 1993

Books Can Help You Dig

People get interested in genealogy for all kinds of reasons. Perhaps Aunt Susie starts reminiscing at a family reunion and your curiosity is aroused. Perhaps you are cleaning out an elderly relative's attic and find a box of clippings. Or you have heard more about inherited conditions and wonder what runs in your family.

Regardless of how your interest is sparked, the next question is where to start. Several how-to books are available. "How to Trace Your Family Tree," by the staff of the American Genealogical Research Institute, and "Finding Your Roots'" by Jeanne Eddy Westin, are available in paperback, and many libraries have Doane's "Searching for Your Ancestors." A recent one is "The Complete Idiot's Guide to Genealogy" by Rose and Ingalls.

Becoming involved with a local genealogical society will put you in touch with others who can help you get started and keep you going.

As you begin to research your roots, digging out names, dates and places, be sure to record the interesting things these people did. Where did they live? What work did they do? How were they affected by the tumultuous times in history: wars, depressions, the western migration?

10 November 1991

Note: Many more good how-to books are available since this column was written.. Look for them at large book stores or in book catalogues.)

Kids Can Help Trace Family

Children can be encouraged to become family historians and genealogists to find out more about their heritage and family traditions. However, it's hard to find a how-to book written on a child's comprehension level.

In the 1970's the Evansville-Vanderburgh School Corp. (Ind.) developed "Tracing and Researching Ancestry" as a teaching unit for middle school classroom use. The program was designed to help students learn methods of genealogical research.

A teacher's guide, introductory filmstrip, student workbook, forms and binder, and a colorful five-generation family chart were developed.

The program encourages interviewing older family members and writing letters to public agencies and individuals. It teaches careful handwriting and other useful academic skills, as well as helping children learn more about their family heritage.

Teachers in Vanderburgh County can use all or parts of this program at little cost, and it is available for nominal expense to anyone outside the county. For more information, contact Curriculum Office, EVSC, 1 SE Ninth St., Evansville, IN 47708.

Indiana and many other states have a 4-H Family Tree or Genealogy project, one of many available, that is another way for children to become involved in genealogy. They need not have been in 4-H before to join a club and work on this project.

To get in touch with the nearest club, contact the Co-operative Extension Service in your area. Adult help is available to show children how to proceed with the project.

I greatly regret that I did not become interested in genealogy while my grandparents were still living. I am still looking for information that would have been available for the asking. Children may lose interest after a time, but the family information they find will be useful to them or other family members later.   15 March 1992

CHAPTER 2

LIBRARIES AND ARCHIVES - WHAT YOU CAN FIND THERE

Library Is Next Step To Research Family

You have looked through the attic and the shoe box of family papers and are ready to take the next step in researching your family. Try the library.

Librarians are great collectors and savers, and people who don't know what to do with their collection of papers often give it to a library.

Find out where the library's genealogy and family history material is located. More and more people are interested in doing family research and libraries often place their pertinent material on separate shelves.

Start by looking in the card catalogue under the surname you are pursuing, as well as key subject headings such as Vital

Records, Cemeteries, or Church Records. Also look for county histories. The older they are, the more helpful they are likely to be. Most libraries have city directories and school yearbooks. Check for the years your ancestor might have been there.

Don't be put off if the card catalogue is now a computer screen. The staff will help you if you get stuck and it won't take long to catch on to its use.

Much of the library material you want may not be listed in the card catalogue. Loose collections of papers may be in the Vertical File, or Manuscript Collection. These could contain helpful hand-copied cemetery inscriptions, newspaper clippings of some notable event, or abbreviated family history material. These items are not suitable to be bound to stand on the shelf, but any one of them could contain information to help in your family search.

Ask if the library has material about organizations your ancestor might have belonged to, such as the Odd Fellows or Germania Maennerchor. Also, find out about any special collections of material relating to family history or genealogy. Willard Library, for example, has eleven microfilm reels of deaths reported in Evansville newspapers from 1928-1981, compiled by Charles H. Browning. Another library might house someone else's collection.

Not all maps are bound in the current atlases. A special map collection would be the place to look for places or water courses not shown on today's map.

Don't overlook the library's photo collection. Your family didn't have to be socially prominent to have been included. There won't be an index to everyone in every photo, so think about occasions or places where your ancestors might have been photographed.

If your ancestor died before the county recorded deaths, his passing might have been noted in the newspaper. These may be on microfilm, or someone might have abstracted the vital records. The paper on which newspapers were printed ages faster than any other item you will look at, so don't be disappointed if you can't find a paper copy of the one you seek.

If you see a microfilm or microfiche reader in the room, ask the librarian if there is a separate list of such holdings; most are not in the card catalogue.

A card file may be kept of people who are researching families, with the surnames being searched, which might put you in touch with a distant cousin with whom you can share information.

If you are going to an out-of-town location, check the "American Library Directory" for the name, address, and phone number of the local library. Write ahead to make sure they will be open when you are there, and include a self-addressed postcard for their easy reply.

You may not find everything you seek at the library, but you are sure to find something to add to your family story. Don't overlook the material that is off the shelf.

29 August 1993

Genealogist's First Commandment:

Thou shalt honor your heritage and pass it on to your family. This includes writing your story and organizing your family history material so someone else can understand it. Don't let what you have discovered die with you.

New England Register Helps Researchers

If you have ancestors from New England or New York, you need to become familiar with the New England Historical and Genealogical Register. Published since 1847, the Register is the largest single source of printed material about early settlers in New England.

The original intent of the journal was to include "biographical memoirs, sketches and notices of New England before 1700; showing from what places in Europe they came, their families there, and their descendants in this country." It also includes many family genealogies, lists of names found in early documents, cemetery inscriptions, town and parish records and business records. Since many New England towns kept records of births, deaths, and marriages from the earliest time, they are more complete than for most other states. Many have been printed in the New England Register.

A four-volume index was compiled for volumes 1-50, listing each name, as well as a separate index to places.

An abridged index to the principal names found in volumes 51 to the present has been published, but does not include each name in the text. A better way to check subsequent issues is by using the index to names and places in the back of each volume. Using it is the best way to make sure you haven't missed a tidbit about your relative.

Even though you may not think your family came from New England or were in North America that early, check the indexes for your ancestor anyway. Some material from other colonial areas has been included, and you may find that your early ancestor married into a New England family.

12 April 1992

Capital Has Links To Your Past

Is your family going to Washington, D.C. to see the sights this summer? Why not make time to search for information about your ancestors?

Genealogists think first of the National Archives when they think of researching in Washington. That's hard to work into a vacation unless the whole family is interested.

Here's a guide to three libraries in which a few hours can be well-spent. Call ahead to be sure they will be open at the time you want to visit.

* **The Library of Congress** at 10 First St. SE on Capital Hill has a large collection of genealogies, local histories and city directories in the Thomas Jefferson Building. Hours are 8:30 a.m. to 9 p.m. Monday through Friday, 8:30 a.m. to 5 p.m. Saturday, and 1 to 5 p.m. Sunday; closed on federal holidays; phone (202)707-5537. Parking is hard to find, but the Metro subway will take you within a few blocks.

* **The National Genealogical Society**, 4527 17th St. N, Arlington, Virignia has a collection of genealogies, family and local histories and source books. Perhaps their collection includes the cemetery or marriages in the area you are researching. Hours are 10 a.m. to 9 p.m. Monday and Wednesday, 10 a.m. to 4 p.m. Friday and Saturday; closed Tuesday, Thursday, Sunday and federal holidays; phone (703)525-0050.

* **National Society Daughters of the American Revolution library**, 1776 D St. NW, Washington, has family histories and genealogies as well as local source material, including documents copied by Daughters of the American Revolution chapter members that are not published elsewhere.

Many libraries have copies of the DAR Library Catalog, which indexes the holdings received through 1986 by title, author and subject. The subject index includes family genealogies.

Hours are 9 a.m. to 4 p.m. Monday through Friday, 1 to 5 p.m. Sunday; phone (202)628-1776. A $5 daily use fee is charged to non-DAR members. Parking is limited on weekdays, so visitors are advised to use the Metro.

All three libraries will send pamphlets explaining how to use their offerings, or you can consult C. S. Neal's "Lest We Forget: Guide to Genealogical Research in the Nation's Capital".

24 May 1992

Genealogist's Second Commandment:

Thou shalt not create fiction when writing about your family. Stick to the facts as you find them; don't make up something just to fill in the blanks.

Get the Whole Family Involved

If you plan a summer visit to any community where your ancestors lived, you might enjoy searching for your family roots along with the rest of your vacation activities. It's a way to bring the past alive for the whole family, but you'll need to plan ahead to get the most out of it.

Some tips:

* Record basic information about the relatives you want to research: dates and places of birth, marriage and death, for example. Sample forms are available in any how-to book, and will help to remind you of what you are looking for.

* Write letters to the places you hope to visit. Prospects include the public library in the county seat where your ancestor lived, the courthouse, and the office of the cemetery where he was buried. To ensure a reply, write early and include a self-addressed stamped envelope (SASE).

Consult a directory of libraries at your local library to find the name and address of the library you want to visit. When you write, ask when it is open. Explain the purpose of your visit and ask whether they have any family genealogies of the surnames you are seeking.

If you are taking young children, remember that they often get bored by research; ask if the library has any children's programs. Perhaps you can time your research to take advantage of them.

Records of marriages, births and deaths, wills and probate records, as well as land transactions and other official business, will most likely be housed in the county courthouse. This is not a place for small children, but teens can often help.

Before you go, find out what records are available for what years, and which office houses them. The "Handy Book for Genealogists" (Everton Publishers, Inc., Logan, UT) lists this information for each county.

Write to each office you plan to visit, explaining what you are looking for. Find out the hours they are open and whether there are any restrictions on the use of the records.

Birth and death records for most of the 1900s can only be searched by the office staff, and you will need a close approximation of the year you need. You may find that the oldest records have been transferred to a local or state historical society.

Children can be a big help in locating tombstones in a strange cemetery. As they help hunt, they may find some things on gravestones that will spark their curiosity. Records of war service are often noted there as well as membership in social or fraternal organizations.

A town cemetery usually will have an office. Start there. The county surveyor's office in the courthouse can help locate a rural cemetery.

If grandparents or other older relatives still live in the community you will visit, your children can ask them to reminisce. Help the children compile lists of questions ahead of time.

You may want to locate the old farmstead or home where your ancestors lived. If the property is no longer in the family, use discretion and courtesy in approaching the occupants. Bear in mind that some people who go back to grandmother's old house are quite disappointed that it no longer looks as they remembered it.

To help children stay involved in this summer adventure, encourage them to keep a journal of the things they see and do. Take along a camera and a small tape recorder as well as a journal.

7 June 1992

'Mug Book' Is Another Source

Once you know where your ancestors were living in the late 1800s and early 1900s, you might find more about them in a county history or "mug book".

Several publishing companies went from county to county, soliciting family material. The families that paid the most got the longest write-ups. If you do not find your family in these publications, it may be because they were unwilling or unable to pay to be included.

Most of the original printings of these books did not index every name, making them hard to use. But many books have been reprinted within the last 25 years by historical and genealogical societies, and some reprints include a more complete index.

Some of the books were completely biographical; others included a history of the county and its townships. Check the table of contents for information about churches, schools and township or town histories. Even though your family may not be in the biographical write-ups, they may be mentioned in other parts of the book.

A cautionary note: If you find an ancestor mentioned, do not assume that everything you read is true. The publishers made no effort to verify anything. The informants may not have known as much as they thought they did, or may have elaborated a bit for the sake of vanity.

One of the best collections of county histories in the Tri-State is curently part of the collection of Willard Library in Evansville. Unigraphics Inc. reprinted dozens of these books from all over the Midwest, and a copy of each was given to the library.

10 May 1992

PERSI Can Be A Genealogist's Best Friend

If you haven't already done so, it's time you got to know a Hoosier named PERSI. PERSI can help you find published information about your family or the area in which they lived.

PERSI, the Periodical Source Index, is the brainchild of the Allen County (Ind.) Public Library Genealogy Department, and was begun in the early 1980's.

The library in Fort Wayne has one of the largest genealogy and family history collections in the US. Among their holdings are hundreds of journals published by genealogical and historical societies all over the world.

Initially the index was conceived as a tool to be used by their staff and patrons to locate articles buried in the magazines of their collection. Fortunately for the rest of us, they soon realized that other libraries might be interested in the index even though they may not have the magazines, and many libraries now have PERSI.

Family historians seem to be most interested in finding their surnames in print, so the first several volumes separated families from places. If more than one family is featured in an article it is indexed under both surnames.

The place index lists states by county, Canadian places, and other countries. Articles are subdivided under the place by the type of record (cemetery, census, marriages, etc.).

The yearly updates and additions since 1986 include families and places in the same volume. Additional journals are being added to their index each year, expanding the scope of PERSI.

An appendix at the back of each volume identifies the four-letter code for each journal. The listing also includes the volume and issue number, followed by the month and year of publication.

So, how do you find a copy of the magazine article, once you have located the reference? After you have determined that the local library, or the computer system to which it is connected, does not have the journal, you can either send for a copy of the article from the organization which published it, or ask your librarian to get a copy through inter-library loan.

"The Genealogist's Address Book" (Genealogical Publishing Co.) can provide the address of the organization, and you can write directly. Send a self-addressed stamped envelope and expect to pay a copy fee, but it probably will be a bit faster than inter-library loan.

Some journals from state and national organizations have published their own indexes. The Illinois State Genealogical Society Quarterly has just compiled a 25-year index to volumes 1-25. The Indiana Magazine of History, published by the Indiana Historical Society, has the same thing. All of these are short-cuts to finding the valuable information published in genealogical and historical society journals, another potentially valuable source in your family search.

16 January 1994

CHAPTER 3

RESEARCHING IN THE COURTHOUSE

Searches Being Restricted

Original records are the ultimate in authority for the family historian. In our searches we are told to go to the court house and find them in the clerk's or recorder's office. But with more and more of us digging for our ancestors, quite a strain is being put on the county offices and on their records.

We seem to be most interested in the oldest records. You know the ones - they are in the books that are falling apart, the edges of the pages are crumbling, and the writing is dim and very nearly indecipherable. Or they are the packet of probate papers that is missing because someone else wanted to keep the original paper with great-grandfather's signature.

Sometimes the earliest records have been transcribed to a card file index. But when you don't find your ancestor where you thought he should be, you wonder whether his entry was missed in the indexing, or whether he never was there at all.

There is a fine line between the public's right to complete access and the official right to restrict access. From the official standpoint, managing old records is an expensive, time consuming, and on-going project.

Marriages, estates, divorces and land transactions of the last fifty years are the ones most used for every-day official business-the kind of business they were elected or appointed to carry on.

But the older records must be housed and preserved, even though they are not used often. Offices are doing various things to try to accommodate both camps.

Some of the oldest, most fragile records are being stored in state and county archives, or regional library repositories where archivists are better trained in the preservation and storage of such things.

Many offices have put the oldest records on microfilm and microfiche, thus keeping the original paper from being further degraded by the atmosphere and human handling. Some offices use printed indexes and compiled copies for first inspection, saving wear and tear on the oldest books.

All of these things cost money, and hardly any county office has that in abundance. Some offices now will provide only certified copies of things which were formerly available for a lower priced photocopy. When photocopying is available, it will cost at least $1.00 per page.

Other measures are being taken that discourage use by the genealogist and historian. Some early marriage records in Illinois, for example, are only available as a certified copy, made for a fee by the clerk. The researcher can no longer casually search the books, looking for the ancestor in question, and hand copy the information found there.

Access to birth and death records from the early 1900's to the present, housed at a state office, have always been restricted from public view, to protect individual privacy, and are available only as a certified copy. The cost of these records from state departments of health has risen rather dramatically in recent years - $5.00 in Indiana, $7.00 in Kansas, and $11.00 in Ohio.

As a researcher, you can work around most of these problems, but before you go to the county clerk's office to do a few hours of research, try these things:

* Check the local library to see whether anyone has copied or indexed the records you want. These are often done by local genealogical or historical societies. When you search this kind of copy you save wear and tear on the original book.

* Check the locality index of your nearest Family History Center, Church of Jesus Christ of Latter-Day Saints, to see if the county records have been microfilmed. If so, they are available for your use at very little cost. Again, you save wear and tear on the original books.

Write or phone the office to see whether they have records for the time period you seek, and when they are open. Ask about their access policy and the cost of having copies made. The clerk cannot change the policy. You may not like all the answers, but at least you will be forewarned.

If you find that the old records you seek are stored elsewhere, you will have saved yourself a fruitless trip.

2 August 1992

Ancestral Wills Provide Insights Into Family History

How long has it been since you read the will of one of your ancestors? Not only do wills provide basic information, they can give interesting hints into family relationships.

The fact that one man left $1,000 to each of the sons of his first marriage and $1 to each of the children of his second wife gives me some sense of the internal dynamics of that family. Even though they all lived in the same community, their relationship must have been strained.

You won't always find surprises when you read a will, but the possibility is there, and you will gain insight into your ancestors in the process.

To locate a will you will need to know where the person died, then you can look in the county office that handles probate matters. In Indiana and Kentucky counties, go to the County Clerk; In Illinois, the Clerk of Circuit Court has these records.

Ask to see the estate index book. If an estate was probated in that county, whether the person wrote a will or not, it should be recorded there, and notations made as to which actions were involved. The index will give references to the books in which these actions were recorded, along with the box and case number for the final probate packet.

In researching probate records, here are some terms to keep in mind:

*   **Administrator and Executor** - both have essentially the same function, but are not quite the same. An administrator is appointed by the court to administer a deceased person's estate. An executor has been named in the will as the person who should see that the provisions of the will are carried out. When you find an individual listed as administrator, you need not look for a will because none was brought to court.

If a person dies intestate (without leaving a valid will) the court appoints an administrator, whereas most wills are written to designate someone who will be executor.

*   **Probate** or **Prove.** After a person dies, a written will is brought into court to prove that is the last will and testament. The date a will is "proved" will be the first date after a death in the process of settling the affairs of the estate. If you don't have an exact death date for your ancestor, this may be your closest estimate of the death date.

*   **Heirs of the body, natural son/daughter.** These terms generally include all lineal descendants of a decedent, and excludes any surviving spouse, adopted children or step-children. People unfamiliar with these terms may wonder whether they refer to a child born out of wedlock. Though it sometimes appears to be used in this way, this is not the legal meaning.

Many more legal terms relating to probate are defined in Val D. Greenwood's "The Researcher's Guide to American Genealogy" (Genealogical Pub. Co., 1990). If you are unsure of the exact meaning of the words and phrases you find, it's always a good idea to look it up rather than guess.

One would hope that the person writing the will would name all his children and his wife, if still living. Unfortunately it isn't always so. I was delighted to find the will written in 1832 by a many-greats grandfather, listing his wife and nine children. But the child I was looking for was included in his statement, "as to the children of my other wife, they have already been given their share". No names, nor indication of the share that was given. So much for finding my 3-greats grandmother there.

We often hope to use a will to establish an approximate date of death, and assume it was written on his/her death bed. Look carefully at the date on the will as well as the date it was brought to court, so you won't be mislead.

1 August 1993

Lack Of Will Creates Only Minor Obstacle For Family Detective

One of the frustrations of the family historian is to look for an ancestor's will but not find it. It would have been the perfect place to find the names of his wife and children.

People have been dying without finishing their legal affairs for a long time, and perhaps your ancestor was among the crowd. But don't despair. The law makes provision for other papers to be generated when a person dies "intestate" and these can be even more useful in your detective search.

If he owned any land, or other property of value, the state decided how it should be distributed. Look in the probate index for a reference to an estate packet. It should contain the pieces of paper required by the court to pass property to heirs.

These are often small bits and pieces (they didn't waste paper like we do today), along with receipts from family members and creditors, and can be very interesting. A detailed inventory and/or bill of sale itemized personal property, even down to spoons and bedcovers.

A final distribution statement should list the heirs and their relationship to the deceased. If not stated, these relationships may be surmised by the amount each received: usually the widow inherited one-third and the children shared the other two-thirds.

If one of these children pre-deceased the parent, but left children of her own, that share was divided among them, and they may be named.

When an underage child was among the heirs, the court appointed a guardian to "guard" the financial interest of this minor heir, until he or she arrived at the age of majority. This created more paper among the court records, and could extend over a number of years if the child was quite young when the parent died.

This guardian may have been the surviving parent, or it may have been some other adult. If the mother remarried, her new husband may have been appointed guardian. A child who was age 14 or older could have petitioned the court to appoint the guardian of his or her choice.

Guardianship records will be in the County Clerk's office and a thick packet of these papers can yield even more information than a will.

Sometimes the only indication of property distribution was recorded in the deed books. Look for the family surname, or the name of one of the heirs, in the Grantor Index after the parent died. You may find a quit claim whereby one or more of the heirs gave up their claim to the land of a parent, in order that the property could be sold and the profits distributed among all the heirs. The index listing may be something like "James Schneider et al (and others) to ......"

To make sure this is the meaning of such a transaction, look back in the deed book for the legal description of the land when it was first purchased by the parent. Compare this description to that of the property that was sold later by the heirs. It should be the same, though the final deed may not have specifically referred to the land as having "belonged to Henry Schneider, deceased."

The papers generated about your ancestor who did not get around to writing his will may seem a bit elusive, but his neglect to do so may tell you more about the family, and will stretch your research skills along the way.

24 October 1993

CHAPTER 4

FEDERAL SOURCES FOR YOUR RESEARCH

Archives Are Key Resource

When you hear about the National Archives of the United States, you probably think of the elegant building on Constitution Avenue in Washington, D.C., where tourists view the Constitution and Declaration of Independence under glass. There is much more to the archives than that, and much of it is valuable to people interested in their family roots.

In 1969, 11 regional archives were established to make federal records more accessible to the public. The Atlanta branch serves Kentucky and the Southeast.

The Chicago branch serves six midwestern states, including Indiana and Illinois. In addition to national records, it houses an extensive microfilm collection of federal court, land and other records for those states.

Of particular interest to Midwest genealogists is the Soundex Index to Naturalizations for District 9, 1840-1950. It covers northern Illinois, northwest Indiana, eastern and southern

Wisconsin and eastern Iowa. This index may help locate an immigrant ancestor.

Unfortunately, such indexes are not available for all parts of the country.

Family historians know how useful the decennial census is in finding ancestors. The archives houses other census schedules as well. Mortality schedules provide vital statistics on everyone who died during the year preceding the census years of 1850, 1860, 1870, and 1880. A partial 1890 special schedule of surviving Union veterans and widows of the Civil War also is useful.

13 October 1991

Genealogist's Third Commandment:

Thou shalt acept all your ancestors as they are found. Not everyone can descend from a nobleman or an Indian princess.

Social Security Records Help

You may think your Social Security file is private -- not accessible to anyone else. That's right in theory, but only while you are living. Social Security records can be used by the family history detective to find information about deceased ancestors and relatives.

A person's Social Security number is used on every job application and as an identifying number for many other purposes, even though that was not the original intent of the government. It can be the key to unlocking valuable information.

Federal records of living people are not available, but upon death that right to privacy ceases. A photocopy of the deceased person's original Form SS-5, "Application for a Social Security Number Card," will give the names of the applicant's parents and name and address of the employer when the applicant applied.

To get a copy, write to Social Security Office of Public Inquiry, 4th Floor, Annex Building M, 6401 Security Blvd., Baltimore, MD 21235. Provide the person's name, Social Security number (if known) and the reason for your request. The fee is $7 if the number is known, $16 otherwise.

The Social Security Death Master Index contains files on 42 million people who had Social Security numbers and whose death was reported to the Social Security Administration. An individual's record gives complete death date, Social Security number, month and year of death, and ZIP codes for the state of residence at death and where death benefits may have been sent.

The master death index is available at libraries with computer access and on CD.

8 December 1991

Census Has Helpful Information

Unless you are completely new to genealogy, someone has surely told you to look in the census to find your ancestors. I am also sure some of you have become quite discouraged when you have tried to find your family there.

Between fading ink, careless handwriting, creative spelling and not knowing where the family was living that year, many family historians give up on trying to use the federal population census.

If the census was created for the use of genealogists, the compilers would have been more careful with their handwriting, and would have copied the entries in alphabetical order. But since its primary purpose is to determine congressional representation, we must work with its imperfections.

The first census was taken in 1790, and the population has been counted every 10 years since. Only heads of households were named until 1850; beginning that year, every person in the home was listed along with age and place of birth.

A printed alphabetical index has been compiled for nearly every state for 1790-1850, making it easier to locate a family in a state, county and township, with the page on the microfilm where they can be found.

Though these printed indexes are not always completely accurate, they can save a lot of time. Remember, however, that some people have always been missed by the census-taker; 1990 was not the first year for an undercount.

Because the population had grown so large by 1850, there are only a few statewide indexes for the later years. It has been a continuing project of individuals and genealogical societies to copy and index single counties for the more recent years, through 1910. The 1920 census will be open to public use in March 1992.

If you had ancestors in Pike County, Ind., you can appreciate the efforts of Clarice June Hale. She has copied and indexed the federal census of Pike County for 1840, 1850, 1860, 1870, 1900, and more recently finished the 1910 census.

Her books list each person living in the county for that year, and include age, birthplace, relationship to the head of the household, etc. Look for copies of the books in Willard and other area libraries.

5 January 1992.

Genealogist's Fourth Commandment:

Thou shalt not brag about your ancestors unless you are willing to give your neighbor equal time to brag about hers. You may be convinced your ancestor's story is fascinating to all your friends, but everyone else thinks the same about their ancestors.

1920 Census Data Available

The 1920 federal census will be opened to the public at the National Archives and its branches this week. Within the next few months, filmed copies will be available at many libraries and for loan.

Willard Library has ordered the microfilm for all of Indiana, Illinois and Kentucky. It will probably be available by mid-to-late summer. For other areas the film may be borrowed through Willard.

The 1920 census consists of 2,076 rolls of population census schedules and 8590 rolls of Soundex index. All states are indexed.

This census contains essentially the same information as the 1900 and 1910 schedules, with these differences: It includes mother tongue of foreign-born, industry and class of worker in addition to occupation; for non-farm mortgaged property, it includes the market value, original amount of mortgage, balance due and interest rate. It does not include date and year of marriage, number of children born to present wife and number born alive in census year, or number of years married.

Film is available for purchase and may be ordered from the Marketing and Fulfillment Branch, (NEPS), National Archives, Washington, DC 20408. A 96-page catalog, The 1920 Federal Population Census, lists the roll number of the population census and Soundex. It is available from the National Archives Trust Fund (NEPS), PO Box 10072, Atlanta, GA 30384. Mail orders for the booklet should include $5.

1 March 1992

Census Records Track Down Ancestors

You've been told the population census is a good place to find information about your ancestors. It sounds complicated and you aren't sure how to go about it. So, where do you start? Here are answers to some basic questions:

* **What will I find in the census?**

Starting in 1790, heads of households were recorded, with children and females as numbers in age categories.

Beginning in 1850, each individual in the household was named, along with age and place of birth. Thereafter, additional information is included: occupations, value of real and personal property, post office address, if the person was married within the previous year.

1880 was even more helpful. Additionally, people were asked the birthplace of their father and mother, marital status, and relationship to the head of the household.

The 1890 census was nearly all destroyed in a warehouse fire.

The month and year of each person's birth was added in 1900 as well as number of years married, how many children a women had borne and how many were still living. If not natural born, the immigration year, number of years in the U.S., and whether they were naturalized was also recorded.

1910 and 1920 are also available, with some variations from what was recorded in 1900.

* **Where can I find the census?**

The hand-written pages filled out by the census takers are available as microfilmed copies. Some libraries have large collections of these, not only for their locality, but also for larger areas. If your library does not have what you want, they can be rented from the National Archives or from other rental programs, by the library staff. Each roll should arrive from two to six weeks after ordering. You will need to use it at the library, on their microfilm reader, within a month after it arrives.

Census film can also be borrowed through the Family History Center, Salt Lake City, Utah.

* What do I need to know to start finding my family?

You need to know where your family was living that year. Knowing that your great-grandfather lived in Randolph County, Indiana in 1870 only eliminates all the other counties in the state. But placing him in Jackson Township should make him much easier to find.

* But I only know he was born in Pennsylvania in 1845. How can I find the county?

Look for an index to the whole state. These are usually available through 1850. For succeeding years, go to the index of an earlier year to see where people of your surname were living. Start by looking in that location first for your ancestor as a child aged 4 or 5.

* Will it be difficult to read the census?

Some are hard and some are not. The census was written decades ago and ink fades, paper gets frayed, and handwriting has changed. In short, the pages probably will take some effort on your part to read correctly. They were written in the order that the census-taker visited the people in his neighborhood, not in alphabetical order. Each line will need to be searched, in order not to overlook the entry you seek.

27 September 1992

Check For Naturalization Records

If you are tracking an immigrant ancestor who came to the US after the Revolutionary War, he may have lived and died as an alien. Most immigrants expected to stay on this side of the ocean, and most started the process of becoming naturalized citizens, but not all completed the paperwork.

Many aliens contributed a great deal to their communities, owned land and fought for their new country. While they may not have become citizens, most of them started the process of naturalization, and the family historian will want to look for all the records to learn more about the real people behind the names.

The naturalization act of 1795 required a person seeking citizenship to reside five years in the United States and one year in the state where he was naturalized, to file a declaration of intention to become a citizen, and to take an oath of allegiance. The person had to be of good moral character, renounce any title of nobility, and forswear allegiance to any foreign sovereign. Though slightly modified from time to time, this is still the basis of the naturalization proceeding.

Congress in 1790 specified that naturalization should take place in a court whose proceedings were recorded, having common law jurisdiction, a seal and a clerk. Although that sounds straightforward, naturalizations have been found among the papers and order books of probate, chancery, circuit, superior and common pleas courts, as well as state supreme courts.

The city police court in Louisville, Kentucky and the Board of County Commissioners in Greene Co., Indiana, both entered at least one petition for naturalization. Congress validated their actions, and those of other unusual courts, after the fact.

The earliest declarations of intent may not give many facts beyond the country or state from which the person emigrated and the year he came to the US.

The form in use from 1906 to 1929 asked for information about age, birth place and date; place and date of embarkation; date of arrival and port of entry; residence in Europe; and physical description (height, weight, complexion, hair and eye color).

Later forms asked for information about his wife and underage children, since they were granted citizenship with the head of household's declaration. The amount of information given on the declaration of intent varied between these two extremes, but it generally will be the most useful to the family detective.

The final naturalization certificate, a copy of which was given to the new citizen, stated the country of former citizenship and the year in which the declaration of intent was filed, but not much more, so the declaration of intent is the part to hunt for in tracking an immigrant ancestor.

Fortunately for the immigrant, but unfortunately for us, the declaration could have been filed anywhere the person happened to be. Most immigrants did not go directly off the boat to the place where they stayed the rest of their lives. They may have spent a few months or years near the port city, and moved several times thereafter.

In 1818, Indiana required an alien to have made a declaration of intention before buying land. This was modified to his intent to become a citizen as soon as possible, and later to mere residence in the U.S. Citizenship was required for homestead land, so this may be your clue to look for naturalization.

A congressional act in 1862 gave citizenship to honorably discharged military veterans. This included northern soldiers in the Civil War, but also those who served in the Mexican, Indian, and Spanish American Wars. Foreign-born men who fought for the Union might have gained citizenship this way.

The researcher will need to backtrack on the immigrant's life as completely as possible in order to search in the most likely places for naturalization records. Place your ancestor in a time and place and use information regarding the citizenship laws in effect at that time.

Many naturalization records have been abstracted and printed in books or journals. The LDS Family History Library has filmed many local naturalization records and these can be located in the locality index on microfiche or computer at the local Family History Library.

"American Naturalization Processes and Procedures 1790-1985", by John J. Newman, gives a concise discussion of the process with a time line of the laws and illustrations of the forms used at different times. It is available from Indiana Historical Society, 315 W. Ohio St., Indianapolis, IN 46202-3299.

In 1941 and 1942 most states participated in a Works Progress Administration project to locate and photocopy naturalization records prior to Sept 1906. A few state projects were completed and are in the National Archives, and most states have at least partial collections. The Indiana records are now in a card-file index in the Indiana State Archives. Other states have begun transfer of naturalization records from state and local courts to the state's archives. Check in all these places.

7 November 1993

Records About Public Land Sales Can Help Locate Missing Ancestor

The lure of cheap land was hard for people to resist. Whether native-born or immigrant, the unclaimed land in the U.S. was a great incentive to many to go where it was located.

The Land Ordinance of 1785, also known as the Northwest Ordinance, outlined a process for granting land to private individuals. Starting first with the Treasury Dept., all the records of public land sales were consolidated in 1936 at the Bureau of Land Management.

We are most familiar with the Homestead Act, first passed by Congress in 1862. There were earlier acts concerning publicly owned land, but this had the most impact on the states west of the Mississippi. Basically the law provided that any citizen over 21 years old could acquire up to 160 acres of public land by living on it for five years and cultivating and improving the land. The only cost was a small filing fee, though land could be bought as a cash sale. Additional homestead laws were essentially modifications on the original act.

Each law specified the process to be used for acquiring the land, and the exceptions that were allowed. The age requirement was waived for Union Army and Navy veterans of at least 14 days service, and they could use their service time to help meet the residency requirement. If the claimant was not a citizen he must have filed his first declaration of intent papers. Women who were 21 were able to claim land in their own names but needed to be able to cultivate the land.

The Land Entry Case Files, now at the National Archives Record Center, Suitland, Maryland, are valuable sources of information about your ancestor. The homesteader answered a lengthy questionnaire about himself, his family, how long he had been on the land, where he had lived previously, his crops, the size of his house, and more. Neighbors were used as witnesses to attest to the validity of the applicant information, and they also filled out questionnaires.

These case files are available from the archives, but you need to do some background work before ordering them. They are filed by case number, not the name of the applicant.

The Bureau of Land Management, 7450 Boston Blvd., Springfield, VA 22153, can provide the case file number, if you provide the legal description of the land, which can be found in the land Patent Books at the county courthouse, or in the tract books in the state land office. Both of these have been microfilmed by the LDS Family History Library, and are in their Locality Index under the heading of United States, Land Records, Bureau of Land Management.

The legal description includes section, township, range, state, base line and meridian number. Don't leave out any of these when you write for the land office name, the type of file or Act under which the land was entered, and the file number. Don't send any money with your request.

The Works Progress Administration in 1941-42 indexed the pre-1908 land records for Alabama, Alaska, Arizona, Florida, Louisiana, Nevada and Utah. A card file of this seven-state-index can be searched by sending the state, county and full name of the land applicant to National Archives, Washington, DC 20409. Don't send money with a search request.

"The Researcher's Guide to American Genealogy" by Val Greenwood (Genealogical Publishing Co., Inc., Baltimore, Maryland) has a good chapter on land records, and "The Source" by Eakle and Cerny (Ancestry Pub. Co., Salt Lake City) has a brief description of each state's records. Both of these will provide an overview to finding land records.

Public domain land was sold from all the United States except the original thirteen, Maine, Vermont, West Virginia, Kentucky, Tennessee, Texas and Hawaii. If your ancestor was an early settler on the expanding frontier, explore the possibility of his buying land from the government. His Land Entry Case file may provide additional information about him and his family.

21 November 1993

CHAPTER 5

PRESERVING YOUR FAMILY HERITAGE

Preserve The Past For Posterity

If you are not making some effort to share what you know about your family with your children and grandchildren, you may be shortchanging them. You may think that you know little that is worth passing on to anyone or that they are not interested in anything you have to say about the past. Think again.

Many young people are interested in knowing more about their ancestors, particularly those who lived far away. The children do not have to be genealogists to be interested in family history.

Here are some ways to foster their interest:

* **Label and describe household articles** such as dishes, quilts and furniture that came from parents or other ancestors. List the previous owners and explain how you came to have it. If it isn't appropriate to fasten a label to the item, photograph it and label the photo in an album.

If you have strong preferences about who should inherit these family heirlooms, include those instructions on the label.

* **Label all your old family photos** with names and approximate dates. Nothing is more frustrating to a family historian than to receive a box of pictures of people who look vaguely familiar, but who aren't named.

* **Write your own story.** Include the facts of where and when you were born, went to school and were married. Add where you have lived and the jobs you have had. And don't forget your history of childhood and adult diseases. Include the same information about your siblings and whom they married.

Start with these basic facts -- but don't stop there. How did your family celebrate holidays and vacations? If you lived through the Depression, or World War II or the Korean War, tell what it was like, both as you remember it and from today's perspective.

Talk into a tape recorder if you don't want to write or type. You may think your youth wasn't terribly exciting, but you have lived through things that are little known to your children and will be quite foreign to your grandchildren.

Doing the above will be appreciated by your family, even if no one is actively interested in recording family data. If you have a budding genealogist in the family, do these additional things as well:

* **Record what you know of your parents:** their full names, including your mother's maiden name, the dates and places of their birth, marriage, death and burial. Record their occupations, illnesses, where they lived and when they lived there, church and social organization memberships, stories about their lives that make them unique and real to those who never knew them. Do the same for your grandparents.

* **Alert your family historian to any family diaries, journals or a Bible** with name entries. If you keep a diary, make sure it will be available for posterity. You may wish to put time limits on how soon it can be opened, but don't consider it of little value.

There are many reasons why adults are reluctant to share their past with their children. They may not be proud of it; there may be some skeletons in the family closet they would rather keep hidden. If you have been reluctant to talk about the past, I hope you will take a chance. You may find those skeletons shrink in importance when they are discussed.

Someone else's indiscretions or bad judgment cannot diminish your worth. The grandfather who deserted his family when he went West may have left behind much pain and hardship, but as time passes, he will evolve into a character that adds a colorful leaf to the family tree.

21 June 1992.

Genealogist's Fifth Commandment:

Thou shalt always start with yourself and work back. You are likely to waste your time if you start with a colonial Virginia planter with the same name as yours and hope he is your ancestor.

Record Stories From the Family

Many of you will visit relatiives during the holidays. This is a good time to record family stories and remembrances of the older generation. Their information can fill gaps in your family history and help make your ancestors real.

The best interviews require planning. Let the person know you will be coming and give some idea of what you wish to discuss. Prepare a list of questions you hope to cover, beginning with easy, non-threatening ones. "When?" and "How?" questions are more useful than those answered with "yes" or "no".

If the subject of your interview does not remember when something occurred, try to relate it to some other event, such as when he started school or was married. Old photos or scrapbooks are good memory-joggers.

An inconspicuous tape recorder is useful -- unless the person absolutely refuses. Use long-play tapes and test your equipment ahead of time.

If you are tempted to tiptoe around sensitive subjects in the family history, remember that you will never know the response until you ask the question. Don't assume it will not be answered.

24 November 1991

Preserve Your Family Papers

It's house-cleaning time and you are once more looking at those family papers and wondering what to do with them. There is your father's 16 x 21-inch high school diploma, the front page of the newspaper announcing the end of World War I, letters from your great-great Aunt Sophie who moved to North Dakota in 1905.

Everyone who has any feel for history has things like these or others tucked away somewhere. What do you do with them? Start by dividing them into three categories:

* Items which have **monetary value or general historic value** should not be stored or restored without professional consultation. A letter from Albert Einstein or commendation from Andrew Jackson is worth something to a collector and can easily be devalued by ignorance or careless handling.

* **Papers of sentimental value** should not be worried about. Greeting cards (unless very old or from a famous person) or crumbling newspapers with special headlines are interesting and curious, but do not have monetary value. Photocopy the newspaper if you wish to refer to it again, but in general don't spend much time or money on its preservation.

* **Papers with family significance**, obituaries, wedding write-ups, marriage license, letters, should be preserved.

We sometimes unwittingly damage things as we handle them. Letters which are folded and unfolded frequently, shuffled against each other, and taken in and out of envelopes with our bare fingers will deteriorate fast. Paper needs protection from the atmosphere, light, heat, and minute bits of body oil on our hands, even from the acid in the paper.

Never do anything to paper which you cannot reverse. Don't laminate, glue, or mend with transparent tape.

If you want to refer to the paper often, or share the content with others, photocopy it, and store the original.

Use clean white cotton gloves or stamp tweezers when handling the original paper, to keep from adding oil and perspiration from your fingers.

If it is folded or rolled, flatten it. Press under weight for several days before doing anything else. Old, brittle, dry paper such as letters or certificates may need extra moisture to keep them from breaking in the process. A vaporizer will help.

Always test the ink on anything to be moistened, for permanency. Rub lightly with a moist cotton swab in an inconspicuous part of the document.

Soiled or dusty paper can be rubbed lightly with an art gum eraser. Use caution on things written in pencil and on brittle paper.

Newspaper clippings that have begun to yellow and become brittle should be treated to stop further deterioration, though they cannot be returned to their original condition. Photocopy them before doing anything else to them.

To deacidify newspaper clippings, dissolve 1 tablet milk of magnesia in one quart of club soda. Place the paper on fiberglass screen (found at a hardware store) and immerse in this solution for one to two hours. Dry overnight between several layers of white paper towel, under uniform weight. Practice on a document that is not important.

When you have flattened and cleaned your items, they will need to be stored properly to prevent further deterioration. Use clear plastic sheet protectors for letters and clippings. Mount them with stamp hinges on acid-free paper unless you want to see both sides. Oversized certificates or diplomas should be stored flat, perhaps in an artist's portfolio.

Two sources of acid free paper, file folders and storage boxes, and ideas for other storage problems are Light Impressions, 439 Monroe Avenue, P.O. Box 940, Rochester, NY 14603, and The Preservation Emporium, P.O. Box 226309, Dept. C, Dallas, TX 75222.　　　　　　　　　　16 August 1992

Collection of Family Photos Belongs in Album, Not Boxes

If you have been waiting for the right time to work on your family photo-album, do it now. The longer you wait the bigger the task becomes, and the less likely you are to do it.

Most of us have started an album, but the majority of our pictures are in boxes and desk drawers, collecting dust and in danger of being scratched.

It's time to do something with the collection of family pictures, and to share them with your children and grand-children. Great-grandfather becomes a much more real person when you can show pictures as you tell stories about him.

You are much more likely to do this if you have preserved and "packaged" your photos.

First of all, edit your collection. Discard those shots where the camera moved, or Aunt Emma had her eyes closed. If you have three shots of Uncle Harry, pick the best. Either discard the rest, or put them in a labeled envelope to share with others. By saving only the best, you will spend less money on album materials, and your collection will be more interesting.

Temperature, humidity and light determine more than anything else how long photos and negatives last. Protecting them from extreme changes is the most important thing. In the attic they may cook in summer and freeze in winter. Basements tend to be damp. Choose a place that is cool and dry and stays that way, such as an inside closet.

Light is especially destructive to color photos but can fade black and white as well. An ultraviolet filter that fits over the photograph will protect a framed color photo which is left out all the time. Even closed albums should not lie where the sun will fall on them regularly.

The mounting or framing materials should be acid-free and non-destructive. Avoid "magnetic" albums which can damage photos. Those labeled "acid-free" are better choices.

Albums with hinged pages will protect pictures from bending and you will want one to which you can add extra pages. Look for shields between the pages so the front of one photo doesn't stick to the photo on the facing page.

Don't use transparent tape to fasten photos. Acid-free mounting corners are available which allow the photo to be removed later.

You will want to label your photos, but don't write on them with ink. If you must write on the back of a photo, use a soft-lead pencil and place the photo on a very hard surface such as glass, to write lightly. Never type on a photo.

A better way to label photos is by writing on the mounting page. The information can be seen without handling the picture.

The best way to ensure that your photos will endure is to preserve the negatives just as carefully as the pictures. Negatives should be stored the same way as prints: in a constantly cool, dry, dark place. Protect them with photo-safe sleeves – polypropylene is good -- using a separate sleeve for each strip of negatives.

Don't cut negative strips into single-frame pieces. It's difficult to have copies made from single negatives.

If you have the only photo of great-grandmother Smith, consider having a copy made by a professional photographer. This will give you the negative and additional copies can be made for other family members. The photographer also may be able to clean up some of the imperfections in the original photo.

If you are unable to find the display and storage items you need, one source is Light Impressions, 439 Monroe Ave., Rochester, NY 14607. A catalogue and free brochures on special photo storage problems are available.

31 January 1993

Holiday Season Is Ideal Time To Collect Family History

The mid-winter holiday season brings more families together than any other time of the year. There is no better time to encourage your family's curiosity about its heritage.

The task of chronicling your family may seem too daunting to begin, but so does a new 1,000-piece jigsaw puzzle. Both are completed with one small piece at a time.

Begin your family history with those of you who are gathered together. Ask those present to write the vital data about themselves: where and when they were born; names of parents; where they went to school; their jobs - where and when; who, where, and when they married, etc. Even the children should be included.

You may be surprised to find how much interest the younger generation has in your family's roots.

I've seen that curiosity at work this year as my family has gone through a dramatic change. The family homestead that has been a special place for six generations of my family is empty. My parents have moved to a nursing home, and we have sorted through and divided up their large collection of family photos and memorabilia.

As these changes have evolved over the past several months, I have been interested in the reactions of the grandchildren. They have shown a great deal of curiosity about the things that have come out of the trunks and closets.

As your family talks about its past, encourage younger people as well as older people to talk about special things. How were holidays celebrated? What remembrances do they have of their parents and grandparents who are no longer living? Assign one or two people to be interviewers and to tape-record the interviews.

One person in the family should be designated as the secretary/historian, to collect the material written by the others, and to keep track of who needs a second reminder. Every family has procrastinators. This can take several months, but don't let people put it off too long.

Enthusiasm wanes when no results seem to come from the project. The assignment for the next gathering could be for people to share pictures from the past with the whole group. Photos draw everyone's interest, and encourage curiosity about the people and activities shown. They also nudge people's memories.

Whether or not your family decides to bring all the information together in a family history book or a scrapbook is not important. The primary purpose is to get started and to do something positive to encourage the curiosity of the younger family members. The older generation owes it to them to help pass on the family's heritage.

19 December 1993

Chapter 6

MISCELLANEOUS RESEARCH TIPS

Queries Help Dig For Roots

If you have been researching your family tree, chances are you have run into a few knots.

Perhaps you've discovered a record of your great-grandfather in Warrick County, Indiana, in 1889, but you can't find his parents or where he came from. It would certainly help to find someone else who is researching the same family.

Hundreds of genealogical societies publish newsletters and quarterlies, and many newspapers have columns such as this one. Most print queries, brief statements of problems, to help readers find others who are looking for the same answers.

A query about a family can be sent to a columnist in the area where the family was living, or it can be sent to a national magazine. Some accept queries at no charge; others charge a fee or require membership in the organization queried.

The Genealogical Helper, published bimonthly by Everton Publishers Inc., lists publications and notes whether queries are accepted.

In writing a query, state clearly what you hope to learn, such as parents' names, a woman's maiden name or the burial place of an ancestor. Include a location (state and county if you know it) and an approximate date or decade.

Your query may explain that you wish to correspond with anyone who is a descendant of your relative. Be sure to include your name and address.

Type or print your question, and let the editor abbreviate. Don't expect your query to appear in print immediately. The editor's deadline may be weeks or months ahead of the publication date. Most columns are limited in space and cannot always include the query immediately.

Another tip: Instead of writing a query about your ancestor John Brown, ask about his second wife, Susannah McGillicuddy. Readers are more likely to recognize an unusual name.

27 October 1991

Read the Fine Print Carefully

I don't know of anyone with family pride who wouldn't be delighted to find a book about his family.

We received an advertisement recently that sounded like just that if I didn't read the fine print very carefully and if I hadn't seen such offers before.

Addressed to my husband, it said he is "invited to examine The Kinsey Family Portfolio," with his name in it. It spoke about the family coat of arms and said the book would answer questions about the earliest Kinsey immigrants, why they left their birthplaces, how they traveled to new lands and the origins and meaning of the Kinsey name.

The portfolio supposedly contains names and addresses of nearly every Kinsey household in the world, along with a family tree chart and place to house the family historical records.

Sounds wonderful, doesn't it? How can we resist paying $30 for something that is "sure to become a treasured Kinsey heirloom"? And there are only a limited number being printed, so we'd better order by the end of the month.

I have seen a book of this sort, under other names. Even without seeing this one, I can tell you it will have:

*   A soft vinyl cover with our surname embossed on the front.

*   Some sketchy information about early Kinsey immigrants (I'm pretty sure we aren't related), brief instructions about searching for one's ancestors, some basics about coats of arms and a design that purports to be the Kinsey coat of arms.

*   Advertisements for glassware, wall plaques, etc. with our name on them, which we can buy.

*   A computer printout of names and addresses of other Kinseys from telephone directories (with no indication of relationship).

*   Some attractively bordered blank pages on which we can record what we already know about the Kinsey family, and a six-generation family chart on which we can fill in names.

I believe it is overpriced and of little value.

This sort of thing has been circulating to many people who have a somewhat unusual surname for at least 15 years, under one guise or another. If you should receive this sort of advertisement, be sure to read the fine print carefully.

29 March 1992

Genealogist's Sixth Commandment:

Thou shalt never use the word of others and pass it off as your own. Stealing words is called plagiarism. Though it's fine to exchange information with others, don't move entire sections of another's research into your own without written permission.

Explore All Possible Sources

Q: My great-grandmother died in 1882, and I don't know her maiden name or where she was married. How can I find this information?

A: The obvious sources won't work for you. The first place one would normally look for a woman's maiden name is her marriage certificate or application, but to find that record you need to know where she was married. Another source is her birth certificate, but without her maiden name it will be hard to find. And she was probably born before births were recorded at the county level.

One basic rule of thumb does apply, however. When you are looking for answers to questions about any of your ancestors, start by listing all the things you already know about her.

*   **In what state or county was she born?** Look for her under her married name in the 1850, 1860, 1870 and 1880 census. Each of these lists her place of birth, and 1880 lists the place of birth for her mother and father. Since any one of these may be in error, look at all of them. Also, note others living in the home, especially old people with another surname. Elderly parents often lived with a daughter. The 1880 census lists the relationship of each person to the head of the household.

*   **What was her church affiliation?** Church records sometimes list member deaths and may include a woman's birth name.

*   **When was she born?** This may be found on her tombstone, and an approximate birth year can be figured from her age on the census.

*   **Where was her first child born?** If this is the same state or county as her birth, her parents may have been living nearby.

*   **Where did her husband grow up?** Where was he living when they married? How might they have met? As you attempt to answer these questions, you may be able to narrow your search to a few counties.

After you have compiled all you know about your ancestor, look for these additional items:

* **An obituary or newspaper account of her death.** It may contain quite a bit of genealogical information.
* **A death record in the county vital records.** When states started keeping death records at a state office, more useful information is available, but some earlier records are kept in county courthouses.
* **Early county histories.** They often include much biographical information about those who lived there.
* **A death certificate for each of her children** who died after 1900 or 1910 should be available, for a fee, from the state health department where they died. This should list father's name and mother's maiden name, along with other valuable genealogical information.
* **Children's marriage applications,** especially marriages late in life. By 1915 or 1920, much more information was recorded about the bride's and groom's parentage, including mother's maiden name. These records are available from the county clerk,
* **Children's baptism or marriage in church records.** They often include the mother's maiden name. Though church records are sometimes hard to find, and some denominations do not record information of a genealogical nature, it is worthwhile trying to locate them.
* If your great-grandfather was in the Civil War or Spanish-American War, he (or his second wife) may have applied for a pension. **Pension applications** often give extensive genealogical information about all marriages and children and should be explored if there is any indication that an ancestor may have been eligible.

19 July 1992

Road Map To Research May Include Twists, Turns

If you are planning to drive to Kansas City, Kansas, for the first time, you may be able to get there without a map, if someone tells you which highway to follow.

But finding Minneapolis, Kansas, may be a different matter. You will waste time and do a lot of muddling around until you consult a map of some kind, to see just where you are going.

The same is true for family history detectives. You can miss clues to your family's story, and make some wrong assumptions unless you locate the places your ancestors were living. A modern highway map should be part of every family historian's basic tool kit.

When you record the place of a birth, marriage or death, the county should be included along with the town and state. A road map is the quickest way to determine this.

If you send a query to a journal or newspaper in South Bend about your ancestors who lived in Posey County, you may not get any response. An atlas would have provided evidence that the query should have been sent some place closer.

When the oral history of your family includes stories of grandfather moving his family to West Branch, Michigan, you may wonder whether this is close to Woodland, where several of his cousins settled, and whether they all moved together, for the same reasons. When the map shows these towns to be over one hundred miles apart, you should look for different reasons, and probably for different years of migration.

But what if your geographical reference cannot be found on a modern map? Don't give up on finding obscure places, whether they are villages or geographical features such as creeks or valleys.

You have found your family in the 1860 census in Washington Twp., Darke Co, Ohio, and their post office address is

Darke P.O. No matter how carefully you look at a present day map, you will not find any town by that name.

The people who lived in Darke in 1860 may have moved away, the buildings eventually were torn down, and now it is a crossroads in a cornfield. Or Darke may now be a thriving town with a different name. Many places have been renamed since 1860.

The question still stands: how do you find obscure place names? Start with a gazetteer, a geographical dictionary, at your library. It may still be called the same name, but be so small that you have not found a map with enough detail to include the place you seek.

Next, try to find an old gazetteer. Many have been published and libraries sometimes have one that was printed before 1900. If your library does not have what you seek, write the state library of the state where you think your town is located. A simple request, always accompanied by a self-addressed stamped envelope, should bring a response.

Old county histories often contain maps with great detail and should be checked carefully.

Old plat maps may have been reprinted by a local historical or genealogical society, or may be found in a large genealogical library such as the Allen County Public Library in Fort Wayne, Indiana. These should provide help in finding villages and sometimes the locations of churches and cemeteries. If you cannot search there, a simple request by mail will probably be answered. They won't take time to wade through a long explanation or a complicated problem, so make your question short and straightforward.

25 October 1992

Family History Takes Root With Sources

Nearly all of us collect something. Stamps and coins have been longtime favorites. For others it may be antiques. The family historian collects information and memorabilia about the family.

Some are most interested in the stories that have been passed down through the generations. They want to sort out just which ancestor is supposed to have married the sea captain, or why great-uncle Arthur moved to North Dakota, but came back five years later.

They aren't obsessed with finding the full names and the dates of the happenings, but want to see their ancestors as characters in the family story.

Others of us are primarily interested in filling in the blanks on the family charts of our direct lineage, and have only moderate interest in finding out about siblings.

Still others are curious about relationships. They know they are cousins to another branch of the family, and want to know how they are related.

Some would like to see their whole family in a big tree form, to see all the family names on the same chart. And a few family historians want to pull together all of these aspects of their family's past, and are actively working on finding out all they can about everyone in their extended family.

Regardless of how mildly or how acutely you have been bitten by the family history bug, you will be finding bits and pieces of information from many places. These may be from other family collectors who share their findings, from an original document, or from the person who experienced the event.

While you are recording the information itself, be sure to add the source. If it is an information-trade from a distant cousin, add his or her name and address and the date you received it. If possible, try to determine where that person got the data.

When the information comes from a book, be sure to note the author's name, complete title, publisher, date, and page number for each bit of data. Also, note in which library you found it. A statement of "the big red Johnson book" may have little meaning five years from now.

If it's a conversation with Aunt Mary, record the date and circumstances of your visit. Also include a short statement of her general state of health, whether what she said seemed accurate, and any items of family memorabilia she had. You may want to return for other information.

You may think this is all too much trouble. You aren't going to write a book but are only having fun collecting things about your family.

One of the most important reasons to document your sources is the fact that you will eventually find two different names or dates for some person or event. You will need to make a judgment as to which is more likely to be correct. Without the source of each, you can only guess.

Hopefully you will eventually get around to writing about part of what you find, either for your own enjoyment or to share with other family members. When you do so, you will become the family expert -- the one others look to for information.   Along with being seen as the expert, you may also be asked where you found your facts or stories. It will be so much easier to answer if you have documented as you go along.

We all hope that our collections will not die with us and that someone else will come along to take up where we left off. You will make this much easier if you leave good source notes along with your collection of paper.

22 November 1992

Professional Researcher Can Help Find Little Pieces to Big Puzzle

The challenge of finding the next puzzle piece provides at least as much satisfaction as viewing the completed jigsaw puzzle.

Family history detectives have much the same feelings, though their puzzle is never quite complete. For many the search is the challenge, and the new bit of information a bonus.

However, every family sleuth eventually faces the frustration of being unable to search in the most likely place for that additional bit of family trivia. When you are unable to travel to Osage County, Kansas, to look in the courthouse or cemetery, and your letters to the county clerk have been unsatisfactory, your next choice may be to hire someone to do the looking for you.

Genealogical researchers are hired for a number of reasons. Some search records that aren't accessible to you, whether it be the courthouse or a library collection. Someone who uses those records often can search faster and more completely.

Sometimes several pieces of information are needed to come to a pertinent conclusion. An experienced researcher may be the best choice to come up with the correct answer.

Having a family tree compiled from many sources, for someone who is not as interested in the chase as in the finished product, will be the most time-consuming and expensive problem for a professional genealogist. Who you hire depends on how complicated your problem is. It will take more experience and knowledge to make a deduction from several sources than to search a deed book.

Libraries and archives can furnish names of researchers familiar with their holdings. A local genealogical society can provide names of members familiar with their area resources. The July/August issue of "Genealogical Helper" (Evertons Pub. Co.) lists these groups by locality.

The Board for Certification of Genealogists; 1307 New Hampshire Ave, NW; Washington, DC 20036, certifies persons doing genealogical research in the United States. They are designated as record specialist (CGRS), lineage specialist (CALS) for help in preparing applications for societies such as DAR or SAR; Certified American Indian Lineage Specialist (CAILS), or genealogist (CG), one who has demonstrated proficiency in using a wide variety of records to compile an accurate, documented genealogy.

The Genealogical Society of the Church of Jesus Christ of Latter-day Saints, Salt Lake City, Utah, accredits researchers in the U.S. and some foreign countries.

Professional researchers, whether certified or not, may be members of the Assn. of Professional Genealogists; 3421 "M" St, NW, Suite 236; Washington, DC 20007. Its member directory is available in many libraries.

Researchers may also advertise in the September/October "Genealogical Helper", according to type of research and area.

Your initial inquiry should state your research request clearly. Ask about experience, qualifications for your problem, and the records to which the researcher has access.

Ask about fees and method of payment. Most will expect at least part payment in advance. State your spending limit clearly. Fees of members of the Assn. of Professional Genealogists range from $10. to more than $35.00 with the average charge being $18. to $20. per hour.

Send all pertinent information for your problem. Include the books and sources you have searched even though you may not have found anything there. Send photocopies rather than original documents. Keep copies of all your correspondence.

A paid researcher may be able to find the missing puzzle pieces and the search is more fun when we find results.

20 December 1992

Letters Help Bridge Gaps in Researching

Some of the steps in tracking your ancestry are harder than others. For example, you suspect that great-grandfather lived in eastern Ohio. If only you could look in the courthouse, you are sure you could find something.

If you can't manage a vacation to that county, don't despair. Write a letter.

Lots of people write letters, but some get more results than others do. The secret is in knowing where to write and how to ask the right questions.

More people get poor results because their questions are poorly stated. Before you write, ask yourself: What do I want to find? A marriage date? A birth date? When your ancestor first came to, or left, an area?

Ask your questions, but don't confuse the issue by adding statements such as, "Send me all you have on the Walker family." An open-ended request like this will land in the wastebasket.

After composing a simple statement of what you seek (no more than one or two questions at a time), the next step is to decide where to send it. A simple request to check the marriage registers of a county should get a response from the office holding those records, provided you give some close approximation of the year.

"The Handy Book for Genealogists" (Everton Publishers: Logan, Utah) lists the office which has the records and the inclusive years, for each county in the United States.

Sometimes the office will charge a fee for searching, particularly in a city with a large population. Usually the search is free, and you pay for the copy they send. If you are lucky they will photocopy the record, but more often they send only certified copies, for a higher fee.

When your request is more complicated, don't expect the office clerk to do the looking. Answering the question of when your ancestor first moved into or left an area will require looking at several records, and making a determination from what is found. You will need to find someone familiar with the land and/or tax records to do your searching.

Write to the library in the county seat, to the area genealogical society, or to the county recorder's office, requesting the name of someone familiar with the records that could search for a fee.

State your request clearly in your first letter to a searcher. List the places you have already looked and what you have found. Be sure to include some limit of the time and money you are willing to invest in this request. Well-organized researchers should let you know whether this is the kind of search they can do, as well as their charges. Every letter you send to either an office, library or searcher should include a self-addressed stamped envelope. Keep a copy of your letter.

A neatly typed, well thought-out letter is most likely to be answered. If you don't have access to a typewriter, write or print neatly, leave wide margins, and keep the letter short. Don't postpone family detective activities because you aren't close to the clues you seek. Letter writing can bring unexpected bonuses.

28 February 1993

Common Names Bring Unusual Challenges

Nearly all of us have a John Brown or a Henry Baker somewhere in our lineage, someone whose name is so common we despair of ever finding more about him.

The problem is particularly acute when he turns up before 1850, when the census listed families by the head of the household only. To add to the problem, you may find two or more people in the same area with the same common name.

While you may never be completely certain which man is your relative, start the process of elimination by finding all you can about everyone of the name you are searching. See if any of the Henry Bakers can be ruled out.

Start by looking for land records. A deed includes a legal description of the land being transferred. Whether this is described as section-township-range or in "meets and bounds" terminology, (so many rods from the center of a stream to a large oak tree, etc.), find some way to locate this on a map of the county. The recorder's office will be able to help you, or at least direct you to the location of maps.

Look first at the grantee deed index, to find when Henry Baker first bought land. Keep looking until you have found every piece of land bought by anyone of this name, and note the description.

Next, look in the grantor index to see when Henry Baker sold land, and match up the legal descriptions. Early land purchases by a married man were usually bought in the man's name only, but the wife was required to sign when it was sold. If you know the name of your Henry's wife, you may be able to eliminate some of the others.

Locating the land may give you some idea of whether the families were connected, or merely living in the same county. If two men's farms were very close together, and a third one on the other side of the county, chances are good that the distant one was not closely related.

Note the signature on the deed. The clerk who recorded the transaction wrote the one in the deed book, not your ancestor. Some, however, signed with an "X", which may be another way of sorting out people of the same name. If the signer used German script or an "X" the clerk usually attempted to copy these eccentricities.

Don't be misled by the addition of "Jr." or "Jun." to a man's name. It did not always mean that Jr. was the son of Henry Baker, Sen. Frequently it meant that he was the younger of two men in the same neighborhood with the same name. They may or may not have been related and often Jun. was dropped when the older person moved away or died.

Checking cemetery records can also help sort out some of the confusion. If a Henry Baker was buried in the Catholic cemetery near where land was owned in that name and your ancestor was not Catholic, you can begin to draw some conclusions.

Early tax records, though difficult to find, often can shed some light. Occasionally the person who recorded the entry added little bits of information, perhaps for his own help in identifying same-name persons. Nothing should be ignored.

No one said it would be easy to find your ancestor with the common name, but don't give up. There may be more clues than you think.

14 March 1993

Think Creatively When Researching Names

A beginning family historian was overheard to say, "It's easy to tell who I'm looking for because everyone in my family spells our name the same way, and they always have. Sometimes in the census I see names that sound like mine, but I'm sure they aren't part of my family because they're spelled differently."

Unfortunately this person is going to get discouraged before she gets very far along in her family searching. A diligent family detective needs to be more imaginative when considering names.

Names were changed for many reasons. Perhaps an immigration official "Americanized" your ancestor's name because the original was too hard to spell or pronounce. Such action creates problems if you are searching the European hometown of great-grandfather.

Other surnames were changed by translating them to the English word meaning the same thing. Schwartz became Black and Zimmerman became Carpenter.

Names tended to remain unchanged when new immigrants stayed in a neighborhood with other new immigrants, and changed most quickly when the newcomers moved into a more "Americanized" community.

Some name changes are not as dramatic. If your ancestor was here in 1820, you may have a somewhat different problem. Many frontiersmen were barely literate. Anyone who has read old letters is aware of the creative spelling and punctuation sometimes used, even with names. It wasn't that they didn't care, but apparently the way the name was spelled was not as important as it is to us today.

Mistakes got into court documents and other public records and became accepted over time. It seems as if some clerks were hired for their ability to write a pretty script, and not their spelling ability. Names were often written the way they sounded, sometimes spelled more than one way in the same document.

When looking through the printed indexes to a census, be sure to look for every imaginable spelling. Imagine you are spelling phonetically. If your ancestors were German, even the first letter can be different. If you don't find Glunt under G, look under K or C. B and P also were interchanged. This problem could be compounded if your ancestor was German, talking to an English clerk, or the reverse.

You may improve your luck in ancestor hunting if you use your imagination and open your mind to other ways in which your family's surname might have been spelled.

28 March 1993

Genealogist's Seventh Commandment:

Thou shalt remember to document every fact you find by writing the source of that information. Failure to keep this commandment will cause much grief later when you can't remember when and where you found it.

Get Organized Now To Simplify Future Research

Deciding how to organize and store things seems to be one of the on-going challenges of living. It's a particular problem for family historians since we collect paper as well as photos, letters and other family material. What to do with them, and how to locate them later, is a continuing challenge.

Start by separating your photos and other precious documents from the information you have copied. Things of permanent value should be stored in some other safe place, not with your research notes.

Information will be easier to find if it is all on 8.5 x 11-inch paper. Those odd-sized slips of paper you have collected can be taped or stapled to full sheets; they will be easier to use and aren't as likely to get lost.

Separate your material into families. This is fine as long as everything on a page pertains to the same family. However, I've been known to put information about more than one family on the same sheet. Then I must either cut the sheet apart, or photocopy it, to have it in two places. If you've done this, next time start a new page for each surname when the information is first copied.

Next, subdivide the material for each family into localities. Location tells you where to look for other information, and can help you decide which family is being referred to.

Finally, your working notes can be sorted by type -- census, land records, etc. -- and numbered. Since you will be collecting material randomly, there doesn't need to be any special order to the paging. You may prefer to leave them un-numbered, with the option of placing later additions into your notes in specific spots.

Write an identification heading in the upper right corner of each sheet: Johnson / Greene Co., Ohio / p. 14. Any time you remove the sheet it will be easy to return to its notebook or file folder location.

Some people store their research notes in file folders, but I think it's more efficient to store them in three-ring binders. If you don't have enough material to warrant a separate binder for each family, use section dividers with tabs and file more than one family in the same notebook.

At the beginning of the material for each family I keep an up-to-date summary sheet, of the kind of information on each page. It's easy to see at a glance which items are still needed.

Also, noting where I have looked unsuccessfully saves duplicated effort. If you have numbered your pages, record that on the summary sheet for quick reference.

Eventually you will find source material for a location that covers more than one family. You may have found printed tombstone inscriptions from a small cemetery where you suspect several of your families are buried, but you don't yet know all the surnames, and you have photocopied the whole cemetery. Or, you have copied all the marriages for your surname from a book of compiled records. Even computer-generated reports and lists create paper to be managed and storing these things presents a somewhat different filing problem.

Use a large three-ring binder with several tabbed dividers labeled Birth, Death, Marriage, Cemeteries, etc. Punch the pages, and you have created your own source book. Label the outside by the general subject: Darke Co., Ohio Records, or Roberts–Flatter–Buckingham Family. Be sure to identify the source of each piece of information you include.

Whether you are a beginner or a long-time family researcher, it's never too late to take control of your paper.

6 June 1993

It's Always a Good Idea To Look At Original Source

When you are the family detective you are pleased to find an index to the census you want to read, or extracted and printed vital records from the courthouse, saving you time.

However, compiled material is seldom completely accurate. Even if you find what you are looking for in the abstracted copy of the records, eventually you should go to the original books and look for yourself. Here's why:

*   **The person who copied the original record may have misinterpreted the name.** That is easy to do when you are trying to decipher an unfamiliar name in old handwriting.

*   **Sometimes the original record includes extra material.** Notes or comments don't always fit in the forms the abstractor used, so they were omitted.

*   **The abstractor may have missed the information you want.** I once found a marriage record which was not in the index to the book; using the date from a family Bible I found it by searching the book page by page.

After a visit to the cemetery, I found one row of stones was skipped entirely in a book of tombstone inscriptions, leaving out the family I was seeking.

*   **You know more about your family than anyone else who looks for them.** You are more likely to recognize names of in-laws and siblings, and can gain more from the original record than the disinterested compiler who puts them all neatly in alphabetical order.

Be sure to search the library for any available compiled source books, but take the next step to look at the original record or location. You may discover information that someone else overlooked.

4 July 1993

Genealogy Society Is Place To Get Help And Inspiration

You will take lessons to improve your golf game or attend a tennis clinic with a professional. You won't start playing bridge without doing some background work; you'll read a book on the subject or seek out an experienced player. The same principle applies when you want to research your family history: get help from a knowledgeable source.

It may seem as if all you have to do is ask Aunt Eleanor for her lifetime accumulation of family data, but that makes you a collector, not a researcher.

I am continually amazed at the hobby genealogists who have no knowledge of whether there is a genealogical society in their area, or if they know about one, have never thought about attending the meetings.

Their thinking often is, "Oh, I don't have any relatives around here, so there's no point in going to that," as though everyone in that society is only researching ancestors who lived in the immediate area.

If you ask a group of family researchers at a genealogical society meeting where they are looking for information, you'll get answers stretching from Kentucky to New York to England and beyond.

Family researchers find quickly that their ancestors didn't stay in one place. Though they may start by checking local sources, their searches soon extend beyond those boundaries.

These people can help in your search also. If you need to track down information about an ancestor in Pennsylvania, for example, you may find that a local researcher has already done work there and can give you help on how to go about finding information there.

In addition to meeting people who may be able to offer suggestions about solving your research problem, getting together regularly with others interested in the same hobby helps to keep you on track.

It's hard to do productive work when you only think about it once in a while. Every time I attend a meeting or go to a genealogy conference, I come back inspired to get back into that problem I've been putting off.

Most societies consider the education of their members as one of their goals and many sponsor all-day conferences with outside experts. Attending one of these is an easy way to learn more about research methods in other locales and to meet people who are also looking for help.

Genealogists come in all types and they are not all trying to trace their lineage back to royalty. Regardless of their current level of expertise, they all started as beginners, knowing little about what to look for and where to find it. You might be surprised at the help others can give in tackling your research problem.

12 September 1993

Detective Work Should Include Walk Down Beaten Path

When starting to do any research, the first step is to survey the literature. Become familiar with the things others have already written on the subject.

This advice is especially true for the family historian-genealogist. It's naive to think you are the first in your family to be curious about the ancestors. A better attitude is to assume that someone, sometime has written something about the family, and your task is to find that information.

Talk to family members to see if any of them know of anything in print. Look next to the material in the Library of Congress. A copy of each copyrighted book has been sent there and they have been publishing lists of genealogies since 1910. "Genealogies in the Library of Congress" was most recently updated in 1992 and is available in most libraries.

Many books and manuscript materials have been sent to the Family History Library in Salt Lake City. The library's computer or fiche can be searched at the local LDS Family History Library for genealogies about your surnames. Filmed copies of the large Salt Lake City holdings can be ordered at your local LDS Library, unless there are copyright restrictions.

The series "Genealogical and Local History Books in Print" by Schreiner-Yantis is available at many libraries. It lists and describes thousands of family histories, with name and address of the publisher or vendor from whom it is available. The index includes references to families in books that have another surname as the main family. Each of the volumes contains a new list of books, so all should be searched.

A query in a national publication such as "Genealogical Helper" (Everton Publishers, Logan, Utah) may locate another family researcher who knows of printed material.

When searching the indexes of these sources, don't forget the families your ancestors married into. You may find a chapter about your Schneider family in a book about the Nelsons.

If a book is found, ask your librarian to help locate a copy through inter-library loan.

2 January 1994

(Update: Many of these data bases , including the LDS site, can be searched on the internet. Newsgroups may also help you locate material about your family that is already in print.)

Genealogist's Eighth Commandment:

Thou shalt show respect for the books and papers that are used in your searching. The records in the courthouse are often fragile and need careful handling.

CHAPTER 7

SPECIAL TOPICS

Indiana Cemeteries Located

If you have ever driven over back roads and tramped through fields looking for an old cemetery, you know the frustration of wondering whether you are looking in the right place, whether it still exists or whether someone has removed the headstones and it is now part of a cornfield.

The Indiana Genealogical Society is undertaking a project that will be of considerable help to family history detectives. The society's first major effort is to locate all the cemeteries in Indiana and to determine whether the tombstone inscriptions have been published.

The survey will locate the cemetery in a township, with legal land description of section, township and range, along with directions for getting there. Family plots on private property are not generally located beside a road and aren't readily seen, so a location will be helpful.

Some cemeteries are known by more than one name, so all known names will be listed, as well as information about whether it is a public, private or church cemetery.

Over the years, individuals as well as historical and genealogical societies have copied cemetery inscriptions. Some are simply typed copies placed in a local library, while others have been included in journals or bound in book form.

The survey project will not record tombstone inscriptions, but will cite the source if they have been compiled.

The Tri-State Genealogical Society has compiled two volumes of cemetery records that include all the known small cemeteries in Vanderburgh County, Indiana, but not the large ones in Evansville.

19 January 1992

(Note: As of January 2000, the Indiana Genealogical Society cemetery index project is still a work in progress. For more information contact the society at P.O. Box 10507, Fort Wayne, IN 46852-0507.)

Civil War Records Available

Where do you start looking for your great-grandfather's Civil War service record? First, was he a Yankee or a Reb, and in which state did he enlist?

To determine his allegiance (North or South), his regimental unit or the state from which he served, check his tombstone or newspaper obituary for clues. War service is sometimes included.

Old county histories often include local regimental lists. He may have been named in newspaper stories during the war about new recruits or wounded. Don't overlook memorabilia that relatives might still have.

George K. Schweitzer's "Civil War Genealogy" is a good resource guide for tracing your Civil War ancestor, with information sources and how to access them.

An eight-volume series by W.H.H. Terrell, "Reports of the Adjutant General of Indiana," lists rosters of officers and enlisted men. Regiment and company are listed separately, giving rank, residence, date of muster and remarks.

The Indiana State Archives in Indianapolis will search its index of those records for a small fee if you do not know the regiment in which your ancestor served.

"Report of the Adjutant General of the State of Kentucky" gives the same kind of information in two series, for both Union and Confederate soldiers. Each volume has its own index.

The Illinois State Archives (Springfield, IL 62756) will search its indexes of men serving in Illinois units.

In addition to all those books, some libraries have the complete set of "War of the Rebellion, Official Records of the Union and Confederate Armies" and "Official Records of the Union and Confederate Navies in the War of the Rebellion." Each is completely indexed.

F.H. Dyer's "Compendium of the War of the Rebellion" includes histories of each regiment, by state, an index of battle names and a chronology of the battles in each state.

Forms for ordering copies of veterans records are available from the National Archives. If you find that your ancestor was injured or captured, the national records will provide more information. Military pension files often provide much genealogical information.

26 April 1992

Genealogist's Ninth Commandment:

Thou shalt always include a self-addressed, stamped envelope with every written request.

Indiana Source Books

If you are searching for information on Indiana ancestors, you may want to consult the series of Indiana Source Books being published by the Indiana Historical Society.

Material originally published in the society's magazine, the Hoosier Genealogist, has been compiled by Ruth Dorrel into the sixth of a series.

The book which includes an everyname index, contains such Indiana genealogical information as marriages; probates, wills and estates; land records; cemeteries and other death records; church records; and passenger lists.

Records from several counties are included in each category, and nearly every Indiana county is included in the complete series. These books do not take the place of a trip to the county courthouse or the local library, but they can provide another way of finding information about your Hoosier ancestors.

5 July 1992

Cherokee List May Help

Someone in every family group has been known as the "story-teller" -- the person who verbally passed on the family's history and ancestry. With all of today's written records we may forget about oral history as a source of information, but for some groups these stories are just as important today as in the past.

If you have Native American ancestry, you will need to look in unique and sometimes hard-to-find places to put your family tree together. For centuries the only records were oral.

Over the years various enrollment programs and census lists have been created. They may be useful, though finding an ancestor on them can be difficult.

One source, created between 1906 and 1910 may help those tracing ancestry in the Eastern Cherokee tribe. During those years the U. S. Court of Claims took applications from 46,000 Eastern Cherokees or their descendants who were eligible to share in a one million dollar judgment in favor of the Cherokees. This payment was to go to all living persons who were members of the Cherokee tribe at the time of the broken treaties of 1835-36 and 1845.

The applicants were from all over the United States. Some were known and accepted Cherokees, but there were also white and black families with strong family traditions of Indian ancestry, as well as many Creeks from southern Alabama who had misunderstood the eligibility criteria. All these people relied strongly on oral tradition to recount their ancestral connection.

These applications, with the decision of acceptance or rejection, were filed in the National Archives. 12 rolls of microfilm designated as M685 are housed in Washington, D.C. and the Federal Records Center in Fort Worth, Texas.

They are also available in eight volumes, "Cherokee by Blood: Records of Eastern Cherokee Ancestry in the U.S. Court of Claims, 1906-1910" by J.W. Jordan (Heritage Books, Inc.).

This series presents detailed abstracts of the applications including numerous verbatim transcriptions of affidavits by the applicants, their families and friends. Since most of the applicants were descendants, and had to prove their descent, the quantity of genealogical data in these volumes is impressive.

The cases were cross-referenced to other family members who also filed claims. Each volume has a complete index, listing both English and Cherokee names.

30 August 1992

Genealogist's Tenth Commandment:

Thou shalt not believe everything you see in print or on the internet. Ask for the source of the information.

Ellis Island Symbolizes Drama of Immigration

Ellis Island has come to symbolize the beginning of a new life, the hope for a golden future, and a chance for freedom for millions of poor and oppressed. It stands beside the Statue of Liberty as the gateway to freedom.

Though few of us began life in the United States with a trip through this immigration center, we have seen pictures of the women in babushkas and men in baggy overcoats. We think we know them.

It's estimated that nearly 17 million immigrants entered this country through Ellis Island from the time it opened on January 1, 1892, until it closed in 1954. Over half the current population of the United States is directly related to those who passed through what was the principal immigration receiving station of that time.

Immigration is synonymous with the settlement of America. The founding of this country by European settlers began a movement of people which ultimately brought 42 million immigrants -- the greatest migration in recorded history.

However, the federal government passed no immigration laws until 1819, and in 1882 finally set standardized immigration requirements, screening, and processing procedures.

Nearly all those who emigrated to the United States between 1820 and 1880 were northwestern Europeans. But those who came into Ellis Island came predominantly from southern and southeastern European countries, including 2.5 million from Italy. Russia sent 1.9 million, followed by all the then-existing countries of Europe.

The facility at Ellis Island was no longer needed after the passage of the "national origins" quota system laws in the 1920's cut the number of new immigrants to a trickle.

In the decade after Ellis Island opened, 3,047,130 immigrants arrived at the port of New York, while only 640,434 came through all other ports of entry. Immigration reached its peak between 1900 and 1910 when 8.7 million arrived nationwide and 78% of them came through New York. Up to 5,000 immigrants every day passed through Ellis Island during the peak years.

Only immigrants coming in steerage (the lowest cost) had to come to Ellis Island. About 10% were cabin passengers, processed on board, and deposited directly to the steamship offices in New York City, avoiding Ellis Island altogether.

In spite of the confusion and turmoil of arriving in a strange land, the most terrifying aspect of Ellis Island was the fear of being deported. All arrivals had to go through physical and mental examinations to determine who was eligible to enter the country and who was to be sent back. About 2% were not admitted.

Processing took days for some, but most immigrants made it through in a few hours. As one journalist of the time reported, "If they could prove they weren't diseased or feeble minded, could support themselves, and knew where they were headed, they quickly moved through the door marked PUSH FOR NEW YORK."

Though unused for over forty years, Ellis Island has been re-opened as a museum and monument to the immigration movement. The goal of the Ellis Island Museum is to capture the human drama that took place there. Half the interpretive space is devoted to telling the story of Ellis Island and the remaining areas portray the immigrant experience.

The William Randolph Hearst Oral History Studio is ready to tape the recollections of immigrants who came through Ellis Island, and the workers who processed them, and will eventually house the most extensive collection of oral histories on immigration in the world.

Though it is hoped that some day a giant computer database will be available to locate any immigrant ancestor who went through Ellis Island, there are not now any immigration or ship's passenger lists located there.

But the island is unique in American history and should be visited to try to understand what our ancestors went through in coming to America.

13 September 1992

Genetic Disease May Infect Family Tree

When we meet a new child in the family we all indulge in the parlor game of speculating which side of the family she or he resembles. We observe eye and hair color to see which inherited traits this child carries. We need to remember that genetic diseases are passed from generation to generation the same as brown eyes and dimples.

There are few families that are not affected by genetic disorders. These may be devastating diseases like cystic fibrosis or sickle-cell anemia, chronic conditions like high blood pressure, or a predisposition to alcoholism or mental illness. Heart disease, diabetes, and cancer all tend to "run in families".

You should not consider yourself doomed to having one of these diseases if a parent or an uncle suffered from it, but you should be aware of the risks.

The family historian/genealogist can play a major part in helping other family members become aware of what runs in their family.

Geneticists are interested in genealogy and genealogists need to be interested in genetics. It is useful for all of us to compile a medical pedigree, but you need not be an experienced genealogist to do so. You only need to be concerned with compiling accurate medical information about your family as far back as your four grandparents.

In addition to causes of death for your parents and grandparents, do the same for their siblings. Your grandfather may have died in an auto accident, but some of his brothers and sisters may have had diabetes or heart attacks.

Each person in a family does not inherit exactly the same genes, so the whole family needs to be considered when compiling your medical inheritance.

Death certificates are one of the easiest places to find accurate causes of death. Since it can be rather expensive to acquire these for all the people involved, check to see if family members already have copies.

Death certificates will include date of death, cause and contributing factors, age at death, length of illness, name of attending physician, funeral home, and place of burial. Some cities and states have death records from the mid-1800's, but more detailed information usually is not available until the early 1900's.

In Indiana, death certificates are available beginning in 1900, from Indiana State Board of Health, 1330 West Michigan St., Indianapolis, 46206. Illinois death records are available from the county clerk beginning in 1877, and after 1916 from the State Department of Public Health, Springfield, Illinois.

Kentucky began registering deaths on January 1, 1911. These are available at Office of Vital Statistics, 275 East Main St., Frankfort, 40621. Check "Handy Book for Genealogists" (Everton Publishers) for specific dates for the county in question. All states will have their own forms for requesting information. Send a self-addressed stamped envelope with your request.

Newspaper obituaries and cemetery records should be searched for any clues about causes of death or state of health prior to death. Be sure to quiz other family members who may remember illnesses or conditions you don't know about.

Most family sheets and pedigree charts do not include space to record causes of death, or information about other health problems. Myra V. Gormley in "Family Diseases -- Are You at Risk" (Baltimore: Genealogical Publishing Co, 1989) shows some ways in which this information can be incorporated in a chart that will be easy to use by both family members and your doctor.

Gormley also lists several dozen physical conditions and characteristics which may be factors in genetically transmitted diseases or conditions, as well as personality and behavioral traits.

8 November 1992

Delay in Recording Ancestor's Birth Can Create Confusion

Nearly everyone today has a birth certificate, or knows where to get one. State and county health departments have been keeping birth records since the early 1900's. But what can you do if your birth was not recorded properly? This sometimes occurred when babies were born at home and the doctor didn't get to the courthouse for awhile. Perhaps the clerk wrote the wrong name, or just called the infant "baby Jones".

We need birth certificates for employment, military enlistment, to receive old-age assistance from Social Security. Our parents and grandparents needed them for some of the same reasons.

In the late 1930's the Indiana legislature empowered county courts to establish birth records for individuals who did not have an official birth record. This may be the place to look for birth information about an ancestor.

In Indiana, these records are in the county clerks office and will be called Birth Records Established by Court, or Delayed Birth Records. These records are considered open to the public, like birth records in the health department.

These court actions began in June, 1941 and continued through 1971. Hundreds were recorded each month in the early 1940's, perhaps for enlistment into the armed forces. Also, many of the early beneficiaries of Social Security would not have had their birth recorded in a county office and this was a substitute.

The court record gives the name of the applicant, his birth date and place, the name and birth place of both his father and mother, his birth order in the family, and the name of the physician or midwife in attendance at his birth.

The index has names listed in partial alphabetical order under the first letter of the surname, but to find Johnson one needs to scan all of the "J" index pages.

Willard Library has an index and 13 rolls of these records for Vanderburgh County, on microfilm. Filmed by the Genealogical Society of Utah in 1980, copies are also available in the Genealogy Division of Indiana State Library, and through the LDS Family History Library branches.

For Posey and Warrick Counties, such records are in the Clerk's Office at the county courthouse.

Illinois has some of the same, but they may be more difficult to find. Start with a letter of inquiry to the office of Clerk of Circuit Court, asking about Births by Court Order.

In Kentucky, the circuit court clerk at the county level, and the Office of Vital Statistics at Frankfort, Kentucky, have some delayed birth records. Start with a letter to the county where your relative might have lived.

If you have looked unsuccessfully in other places for your ancestors birth information, it may be recorded as a Delayed Birth Record.

6 December 1992

Illinois' IRAD System Has Little-Used Data

If you have Illinois ancestors and haven't become acquainted with IRAD, short for Illinois Regional Archives Depository system, you may be missing a chance to find some little-used records

In 1976 the Illinois State Archives, in conjunction with six state universities, began the system to create depositories throughout the state, for local government records. It is designed to help county offices preserve deteriorating records and to make them more readily accessible.

Not all county records have been transferred or filmed. Some important, often used, records have been filmed and the originals remain in the county. Others, particularly very early and seldom used records, have been transferred but film copies kept in the county.

The universities which house records for counties in their area are Northern Illinois Univ. at Dekalb, Western Illinois Univ. at Macomb, Illinois State Univ. at Normal, Sangamon State Univ. at Springfield, Eastern Illinois Univ. at Charleston, and Southern Illinois Univ. at Carbondale.

Chicago records and some from Cook county have been added to the system and are housed at Northeastern Illinois Univ. in Chicago.

There are both advantages and disadvantages to this dispersal of county archival material, from the standpoint of the family history researcher. The university library provides staff to preserve the old records, and they know what is available. Though most courthouse clerks are familiar with most of their records, they are often too busy to be of much help to novice genealogists. Librarians assume this as part of their job.

On the other hand, not all of the records of a county will be available in the regional archives library. Each county has decided which records it wishes to transfer and this varies considerably from county to county.

One would expect to look for birth, marriage, divorce and death records in a county office, as well as probate and land transactions. Naturalizations, cemetery records, poor farm lists, voter registrations, coroner's inquests, and professional registers of doctors, midwives, dentists, and veterinarians may also be places where your ancestors are mentioned.

To find out which of these are housed in the IRAD system, for the county of your interest, write to Information Services/IRAD, Illinois State Archives, Springfield, IL 62756. (Telephone: (217)785-1266. Please limit your request to five (5) counties at a time.

Additional help is available by mail. The library staff will search a county's records for two people per request. The above address will provide a Research Policy Sheet to help in mail requests.   3 January 1993

W.P.A. Records - A Valuable Source For Family Detective

The W.P.A., or Works Progress Administration, was part of Franklin D. Roosevelt's alphabet-soup of government programs designed to put millions of people back to work during the depression of the 1930's.

About 8.5 million Americans worked on W.P.A. projects. They built roads and bridges, along with some of the parks and public buildings we still use.

There are also less well-known projects on which unemployed secretaries, teachers and scholars worked. They inventoried public records and compiled indexes for forty of the then forty-eight states -- all but Connecticut, Delaware, Maine, Maryland, Ohio, Pennsylvania, South Carolina, and Vermont.

Each participating state published inventories or guides to the vital statistics records available for various counties, cities and towns within it's boundaries. These list names and dates, as well as where the records were filed, at the time the inventory was taken.

Composite name indexes also were compiled for some counties which cross-referenced names included in county histories and atlases. This is especially useful since most old county histories originally were not published with indexes of all names.

Vital records normally include birth, death and marriage records and these are most commonly included in the W.P.A. inventories. In addition, church records were inventoried in some places, as well as cemetery and burials, military, and naturalization records.

Copies of these inventories are available at larger libraries and historical societies. Typed copies are often available in libraries of the county of the inventory. Willard Library has copies of the inventories for Vanderburgh and surrounding counties.

The L.D.S. Family History Library has photocopied many of these indexes and inventories, making them available to all researchers.

Changes have occurred in how and where some of these records are kept, so some of the original books and papers used to create the inventories may be hard to locate. But finding a name here indicates that a record existed at one time and can give helpful clues in locating the original.

The family history detective who is looking for another place to search should not overlook the possibility that his ancestor was included in a W.P.A. index.

17 January 1993

International Index Can Be Valuable Source in Researching Family

If you haven't been introduced to the International Genealogical Index you are missing out on a possible source for family information. But you need to be aware of its limitations as well as its advantages.

The index is a huge data bank of names and information which has been compiled by members of the Church of Jesus Christ of Latter-Day Saints. People who are deceased, both church members and non-members, are included.

Some of the information has been extracted from primary sources such as church registers, family Bibles, wills, population census, and vital records. Other information comes from the family group sheets that have been submitted by church members over the past 50 years.

The data have been sorted according to the state or country in which the event occurred, then arranged in a list that is approximately alphabetical. For example, Blacker, Blocher and Blocker are all thrown together and arranged alphabetically by the first name of an individual. This is useful because names are sometimes written incorrectly.

The entry may include an individual's birth date, marriage date and name of spouse, or the fact that he was a child of a man or a couple.

Accompanying code letters indicate whether the information came from an extraction or from a member submission. If from an extraction, the film can be ordered from Salt Lake City and the complete record can be checked to see what else might be included.

If the index information came from a member it is possible to determine the year it was submitted. For a small fee you can order a photocopy which should include the name and address of the submitter, and sometimes their source for the information.

All this sounds really helpful but some of the information may not be completely accurate. Since incorrect data may look just as good to the uninformed searcher as the real thing, use some caution when using information from the IGI.

In the last few years a concerted effort has been made to check the accuracy of early submissions, and many corrections have been added. Unfortunately most incorrect entries have not been deleted, so there may be multiple entries for the same person and event, each one a bit different. In this case you need to look at the source of each entry to determine which is most likely to be correct.

The index is available on microfiche and on CD RAM disks for the computer. The computer can quickly tell you the source of the information. Stake Family History Libraries have it in both forms; Willard and some other libraries have one or the other.

New extractions and submissions are being added continually to the IGI data base. If you used it ten years ago, perhaps it's time to check it again for new family information from sources that have recently been filmed, and to find out who else is researching your family.

14 February 1993

Cemetery May Hold Wealth Of Information

Cemeteries may seem like strange places to spend an afternoon, but family historians know the treasures that can be found there. Every cemetery will be looking its best for Memorial Day, so now is the time to go looking.

Be prepared before you leave home. Grass clippers or pruning shears will be helpful if you plan to visit a neglected cemetery; a trowel (used sparingly) may help you read a date that is buried because the stone sank below ground-level.

Though mosquitoes and chiggers may not be abundant yet, its a good idea to take along insect repellent. Sturdy shoes and long pants are good protection against snakes and poison ivy.

Visit the cemetery with a friend. No one expects to be assaulted, but you might get locked in a cemetery, fall into a hole or get injured in some other way. Rural cemeteries have been know to be inhabited by snakes or small animals you don't want to meet alone. Besides, half the fun of discovery is in sharing with someone.

Don't do anything to damage a tombstone but take along some tools to help decipher the inscriptions. Chalk or charcoal, rubbed flat side down across either raised or indented characters can help make inscriptions more readable. Talc in an aerosol can, sprayed onto the face of a stone, then wiped off the high spots, may help also. Lichens and moss may need to be removed with a stiff-bristled brush. Don't use a wire brush - it can damage old stones.

If you plan to photograph the tombstones you find, a Polaroid camera will let you know immediately whether you got what you wanted.

In addition to taking photos, write down all the information you find, just as you find it. If death dates are given along with age in years, months and days, write it that way. Write abbreviations only if the original is that way.

Look beyond the obvious name and dates for symbols relating to fraternal organizations, religious groups or military units. If you find words or symbols you don't understand, sketch them as accurately as you can to be researched later.

Note the placement and shape of the stone in relation to those around it. A family plot with multiple graves may hold clues to other family members you don't yet know about.

Do other graves in the same cemetery have the same surname? You may not yet know how they are related, but the information can provide clues.

In addition to the tombstone information, some cemeteries keep burial records. Finding them will be your next step to expanded family knowledge.

Government-owned cemeteries, such as those maintained by cities or military burial grounds, maintained by the federal government will have burial records.

Church owned cemeteries adjacent to a building, where members are buried, may have records kept by the congregation, depending on the denomination. However, many churches have disbanded and the building is gone. Finding records that might have been kept at one time will be more difficult.

Cemeteries owned by religious bodies, but not affiliated with a specific congregation may have records at a church archive.

Cemeteries owned by a funeral home, will have burial records as part of their business records. Availability will depend on company policy.

The family plot on private property is the least likely to have any burial records. Most of these are no longer being used, but some are still maintained. Some families have formed associations to keep up the family cemetery.

Some missing pieces to your family puzzle may be waiting were your ancestors were buried.

9 May 1993

Help Now Available For Russian Seekers

The new openness between the United States and the former USSR has extended into the realm of the family historian. RAGAS, the Russian-American Genealogical Archival Service, can aid Americas who are searching for information about their Russian ancestors, and archives in Russia where information might be housed.

Whether the family researcher is looking for a document, or wants to contact family members still living in Russia, a procedure has been established to help.

Through the cooperation of the National Archives Volunteer Association and the Archives of Russia, AROS, bilingual forms have been devised for processing requests. From a slow start in 1992, the staffs on both sides are becoming more efficient in the transfer of information.

Communication during the first few months depended on mail, fax and traveling friends, but a computer system has now been set up, and the two groups can communicate with electronic mail.

The Russian staff have been reported to be highly skilled and interested in finding answers for people's questions. Though many of them are not trained in genealogical research, and finding aids are just now being developed to help locate their records, answers are coming back to people.

The project began in Moscow and has been extended to important regional archives in Kiev, Lvov, Kamenetz-Podolsky, Cherkassy, Kharkov, and others in the Ukraine and with the central archive in Minsk, Belarus.

Anyone wishing to use the service should fill out a request form available from RAGAS, P.O. Box 236, Glen Echo, MD 20812. To search for a single document, such as birth or marriage, request "Specific Record Form". A nonrefundable search fee of $22. should be sent with the completed form.

For a fuller genealogical search that may involve linking generations or linking family members within a generation, request the "Fuller Genealogical Search Form". This search fee is $50.

A request received by RAGAS in Washington is forwarded by electronic mail to AROS. There it is translated, and the request is analyzed to determine the exact geographical location, in administrative divisions, both in czarist times and in the former Soviet Union.

AROS then composes and sends letters with specific details of the request to the appropriate regional or local archive, and to the current ZAGS (civil vital records) office.

At this point many problems slow the finding process. Many smaller archives don't know what they have and records have not yet been systematically organized. The Russian archivists are learning about their records as they look for answers to Americans' questions.

The answers sent back to AROS are compiled into a final report and translated into English. A computer version is transmitted by electronic mail to the American side of RAGAS at the National Archives, while a "hard" copy is carried back by a returning traveler, then sent on to the American requester.

The whole process takes several months, but for Americans eager to know more about their Russian ancestry, after years of thinking the records would never be available, the wait may be worthwhile.

In addition to helping individuals, this cooperative effort may pay other dividends in the study of history and sociology, in medical research and in the use of genealogical databases for academic research.

RAGAS is bringing in money to the newly independent archives in Russia, Ukraine and Belarus, and may help them survive in a time of great change.

23 May 1993

World War I Draft Records Provide Details About Male Ancestors

If you are looking for family members who may have served as soldiers, you may be thinking of Revolutionary and Civil War records. Anyone who has examined the contents of a pension file for either of these realizes they can be a gold mine of information

But, it's likely that few men in your family served in either of these wars, and even if they did, they may not have drawn a pension.

A more inclusive, though less detailed, source of information about male ancestors can be found in the draft records from World War I. At that time 24 million men born between 1873 and 1900 were required to register for the draft.

Three registration periods are included. On June 5, 1917 all men between the ages of 21 and 31 were registered. Men who became 21 between that date and June 5, 1918 were registered a year later, with a follow-up on August 24, 1918. Finally on September 12, 1918 all men between the ages of 18 and 21, and those 31 to 45 years of age were registered.

Aliens were required to register, but could request an exemption from military service on grounds of conflicting allegiance.

As in recent years, men registered where they lived. In rural areas and small towns, one Selective Service Board served the whole county, but in large cities there may have been more than one. To find the draft registration for your World War I era ancestor, you will need to know where he was living in 1917-1918.

Draft registration might include date and place of birth, occupation, residence at time of registration, and physical description of the registrant. If he were foreign born, it would tell whether he had been naturalized.

World War I draft registration records are housed at the National Archives-Atlanta Branch, 1557 St. Joseph Ave., East Point, Georgia, 30344. Researchers may go there in person, or may request forms for searching by the staff. A separate form is needed for each person, with a $5.00 search fee for each.

If your ancestor lived in one of the 28 largest cities for which there was more than one Selective Service Board, a street address or ward number will be needed. If you don't already know that location, the 1910 or 1920 census (for which Soundex indexes are available) or city directories may help.

If you are curious about the hair or eye color, or height of an ancestor this is a way to find out. For someone wanting to find the birth place of an immigrant ancestor, this record should not be overlooked. It may tell only the country, but additional information might be there. It can also give you clues about when to look for naturalization papers.

20 June 1993

(P.S.: The World War I draft registration card index is now available on microfilm through the LDS Family History Library. Ask for help ordering the right film at your nearest Family History Center.)

Several Events Celebrate Anniversary of Historic Path To the West

The study of history takes on a personal dimension when you discover that your own ancestors were part of the events recorded in the history book.

Most of us descend from people who were part of the migration west. Your direct ancestry may have stopped in Kentucky or Illinois, but many of their relatives kept on moving. They were looking for unclaimed farmland, fewer neighbors, a chance to strike it rich or looking for a more exciting life.

Nearly all joined others headed in the same direction, following a trail first used by explorers and fur traders. We know the romanticized movie and television stories of a wagon train trip aren't what it was like, but it's hard for us to imagine the real thing.

1993 was designated as the sesquicentennial of the Oregon Trail. Beginning near Independence, Missouri, this 2,000 mile "highway" was trekked by nearly 5,000 midwesterners heading from the Mississippi Valley to the fertile Willamette Valley of western Oregon between 1843 and 1846.

Though it was first used by fur traders in 1811, and continued in use into the twentieth century, the 1840's saw the largest numbers use it to find their way to the northwest.

States and communities along the way celebrated with events and activities during this year. The departments of tourism of Missouri, Kansas, Nebraska, Wyoming, Idaho and Oregon can provide details.

Though the Oregon Trail is not followed closely by modern highways, deeply rutted remnants are still visible in some spots of Nebraska and Wyoming.

At The Dalles, on the Oregon side of the Columbia River, special activities enable visitors to ponder the decisions the pioneers had to make there, as it was the starting point for the last leg of the journey. By the time they reached The Dalles most were exhausted and out of funds, low on supplies and grieving for those they had buried along the trail. The Dalles Convention and Visitors Bureau toll-free number is 800-255-3385.

If any of your ancestors trekked West on this famous trail, and you would like to trace where they settled, "Donation Land Claim Books" lists thousands of names of those filing for land at the end of the trail. It was published in six volumes by the Genealogical Forum of Oregon (1410 S.W. Morrison, Rm. 812, Portland, OR).

Other places in Oregon holding pertinent records are Oregon Historical Society, 1200 S.W. Park St., Portland; and Oregon State Archives, 800 Summer, N.E., Salem.

If you can't leave home this summer, the second best way of experiencing history is through the words of those who did. "Covered Wagon Women" is a 10-volume series, reprinting diaries of those who made the Oregon Trail journey. The editor is Kenneth L. Holmes; the Arthur H. Cook Co. (P.O. Box 14707, Spokane, WA 99214) distributes the books.

Searching for the personal facts of your ancestors is only the first step in family history. Learning more about the historical events of their times helps us all see our ancestors as real people.

18 July 1993

Help For Genealogists Seeking North Carolina Ancestors

If you're trying to track down an ancestor who moved to North Carolina you might be tempted to despair.

There were no major immigration ports in the state, so you won't find immigration records and it's likely he lived in some other state before he moved to North Carolina.

Many Pennsylvanians went south into the Shenandoah Valley of Virginia and then into North Carolina. The more they moved, the harder they are to find in the records.

Many of these movers were Scotch-Irish, who seemed to have little regard for county bureaucracies. They didn't spend much time with technicalities like recording deeds and marriages, and moved on when their neighbors lived too close. Their Baptist churches didn't keep parish records to any extent.

Obviously, these are generalities that aren't true for every North Carolinian, but there is enough truth to create some special genealogical problems when you are looking for Scotch-Irish pioneers.

Several publications are available to help you research in the tar-heel state. Dr. George Schweitzer, nationally known speaker and author, has compiled one of the best how-to books available. "North Carolina Genealogical Research" is available from the author at 407 Regent Ct., Knoxville, TN 37923 for $12.

Schweitzer gives some history of the settlement of the state, and includes chapters on types of records, record locations, county listings of records available, as well as a good discussion of what can be found at the North Carolina State Archives.

The Family History Library has published a research outline for North Carolina. It includes addresses for the major libraries and archives of the state, a bibliography of books on the history of North Carolina, cemetery records and church records.

The 11-page booklet is part of a series of research outlines covering each of the states and may be ordered by sending $1 for any two states to the Family History Library, 35 N. West Temple Street, Salt Lake City, UT 84150.

If you think your ancestor or his father might have died in North Carolina, "North Carolina Wills: A Testator Index, 1665-1900", by Thornton W. Mitchell could be helpful. It is a newly published index to more than 75,000 people who died and left wills in North Carolina between 1665-1900. This does not abstract the wills, but tells where to find them.

While not a complete probate index, this will help find people who left a will. The book may be ordered from Genealogical Publishing Co. for $49.50. (Perhaps this would be a good book for your genealogical society to buy with their book acquisition funds. Let your society know you want it put on the list.)

The best way to begin researching in a state that is new to you is to read someone else's guide to that state's records. Each state is a little different than the next and much time and frustration can be saved by doing some background work first.

15 August 1993

Tracing Kentucky Family Means Understanding Commonwealth Law

Whether you call it the Bluegrass State, the Dark and Bloody Ground, or My Old Kentucky Home, many family lines trace to ancestors who came through the Commonwealth of Kentucky. They came from Virginia and North Carolina, and eventually many moved on to Missouri, Illinois and Indiana.

Looking for your Kentucky origins will be somewhat different than researching in mid-west states.

Kentucky patterned much of her way of doing official business after her home state of Virginia. Land was not surveyed in an orderly grid of sections and townships. Instead, it is still described in terms of water courses and landmarks -- so many rods or chains from the black oak tree to the stump marker. Locating such parcels of land takes a different set of skills and understandings.

Whether you are a beginner in Kentucky research, or have been muddling around there for some time, "Kentucky Ancestry: A Guide to Genealogical and Historical Research" by Roseann R. Hogan will be a good addition to your basic library. In addition to general information about the records and archives where one should start, the book gives a county-by-county list of where to find original and microfilmed records. Special emphasis is placed on women and African-American families.

Exceptions in Kentucky law are discussed, as well as the Virginia origins which influenced Kentucky legislation and practice.

The book is available from Ancestry, P.O.Box 476, Salt Lake City, UT 84110; $19.95 plus $2.50 postage.

The first two federal censuses of Kentucky are no longer in existence, but a 1790 census for Kentucky has been reconstructed from tax lists. "First Census of Kentucky 1790", by Charles B. Heineman, covers the nine counties that comprised the entire state at that time. It includes the names of each of the 9,000 taxpayers and the county in which they lived. Though it does not list every person in the household, it will locate families with the surname being researched. The book is available from Genealogical Publishing Co., Baltimore, MD.

Another reference which may help with your Kentucky research is "Entries and Deeds, Old Kentucky", by Willard R. Jillson. This book provides an alphabetical index to Kentucky wills from 1769-1850 and to those who received or bought land; it draws material from the earliest records, deeds, and military warrants. Virginia used Kentucky land to pay her Revolutionary War veterans, and finding one of your ancestors as a warrantee may help trace him back to his home state. The book is available from Genealogical Publishing So., Baltimore, MD.

5 December 1993

Golden Rule for Genealogists:

Share family information with others as you would have others share with you.

CHAPTER 8

QUERIES

27 Oct 1991: Seek lineage of Mrs. Hiram KNIGHT (nee Mahala WILLIS) b. 19 Feb 1843 Pike Co., IN. Father was Philip WILLIS, b. 1819 in NC, mother was Mary (Mary Jane BATTLES?) b. 1827 VA. Send information to Mary Jane Steele, 1916 Bellemeade Ave., Evansville, IN 47714.

5 Jan 1992: Seek ancestry of Maria BINDER ZISS LANGHORST, b. 1831 (?) Nassau, Germany; died 22 Dec 1886; married Christian ZISS, 19 Mar 1857; children, Christian, Louise, Anna. She was widowed and married 2) Henry LANGHORST who lived at 1110 W. Illinois St., Evansville. Send information to Helen Holtz, 1613 Washington Ave., Evansville IN 47714.

5 Jan 1992: Researching all WATHEN families. Newsletter, reunions: wish to locate all descendants of John and Susannah WATHEN, Maryland, 1670. Carol Collins, 2201 Riverside Drive, South Bend, IN 46616-2151.

5 Jan 1992: Wish information of Leona Inez WAY, b. 1902, daughter of Walter J. and Barbara Way of Otwell, IN. Worked telephone Company and Evansville Printing Corp., Evansville; died Evansville nursing home. Claude Way, 813 Eisenhower Circle, Vincennes, IN 47591.

16 Feb 1992: Seek parentage of Harriet Jane (WEST) PARKER, b. 11 Oct 1832. Mother was SCALES. Send information to Mary Ann (Roy) Julian, P.O. Box 677, Spurgeon, IN 47584.

16 Feb 1992: Researching Jacob REINHART family. Rosella Regina REINHART, b. 23 Oct 1894, daughter of Otto REINHART; mar. Edward BITTNER; d. 22 Mar 1966. Wish information on her siblings and children. Norma Wilhite, 740 E. Broadway, Princeton, IN 47670.

16 Feb 1992: Wish information on ancestry and descendants of Johnston and Mary Ann (ALMON) MOUTRAY; lived Robb Twp., Posey Co., IN. Dau. was Ruth Ann MOUTRAY, mar. August COMPTON, b. 1856. Mary Jane Wildman, P.O. Box 15, Cannelburg, IN 47519.

1 Mar 1992: Wish to locate descendants of children of John W. and Nora (DODD) WARDRIP: Maud May, b. Evansville, mar. 1905 to John L. JONES; Bessie, b. 10 Oct 1890 in Evansville, mar. 1908 to Norbert G. GUFFEY; Harry Edward WARDRIP, b. 23 Sept 1892 Evansville, mar. 1915 to Josephine "Joyce" PHILLIPS. Dala Jo McDaniel-Cornett, 6700 Dixie Bee Road, No. 21, Terre Haute, IN 47802.

29 Mar 1992: Wish to identify a photo labeled "Loyal Women's Bible Class- 1927; may have been German Methodist. Contact Elizabeth A. Brock, 705 N. Main, Winnsboro, TX 75494-2503, if you know anything about this group.

29 Mar 1992: Seek descendants of August GUENTHER, b. Germany, emigrated ca. 1850, to Vanderburgh Co., IN; mar. Carolyn HOFMEISTER (where and when?). Children: William, b. 1856; Edward, b. 1862; Lewis, b. 1864; John, b. 1867; Franklin, b. 1869; Albert, b. 1872. Billie Shelton, Rt 1, Box 141-A, Laneville, TX 75667.

12 Apr 1992: Seek parentage of Charles ROSE who was living in Wabash Co., IL in 1840. Was Lewis ROSE who was living Mount Carmel, Wabash Co., IL in 1830 his father? Where was Lewis ROSE in 1840? Albert Rose, 9720 New Harmony-Princeton Rd., Poseyville, IN 47633.

12 Apr 1992: Seek parentage of Gottlieb Wilhelm BAUMANN, b. 1849 in Switzerland; came to Indiana ca. 1853; d. Evansville 1899; mar. Amelia REICHEL/REICHFELT. Elizabeth Brock, 705 N. Main, Winnsboro TX 75494-2503.

26 Apr 1992: Seek information about William SCHORNHORST, b. 1843 in Germany, not mentioned in father's will (did he die young?); Caroline SCHORNHORST, b. 1845 in Gibson Co., Ind. Their parents were David and Louise (NIEDERHAUS) SCHORNHORST. Sue Hebbeler, 110 W. Maryland St., Evansville, IN 47710.

10 May 1992: Researching SHELTON family who moved to Southern Illinois by way of Kentucky and Virginia: need information on Wm. and Elizabeth RAMSEY, Union Co., KY, whose dau. Margaret mar. Wm. J. Shelton in 1831 (he died 1860 near Poole, KY). Also wish information on Marion SHELTON, son of Wm. J. and Elizabeth (Ramsey) Shelton. Looking for book by Elijah Shelton on the Shelton family. Bill Shelton, P.O. Box 600, Olney, IL 62450.

10 May 1992: Compiling information on the McCUTCHAN family. Wish to correspond with anyone having family records, diaries, letters, etc. before 1900. Bill McCutchan, 10351 Browning Rd., Evansville, IN 47711.

24 May 1992: Seek information about Frederick and Catherine (STEINER) STULL/STOLL family, living in Leavenworth, IN about 1850. Sons were William, Frederick, Label, and John. Mary (STULL) Erdley, 588 Forest Park Dr., Newburgh, IN 47630.

24 May 1992: Need siblings and parents of Malinda GOLIHARE, born in Burksville, KY about 1850, married Scott HUGHES, died in Pike County, IN after 1917. Son was Hershall Hughes (1877-1917). Were there other children? DeAnne Kinsey, 3030 Curry Lane, Carmel, IN 46033.

21 June 1992: Seeking information about David DOWNEN, b. about 1835, probably Mount Vernon, IN; mar. Celiann OLIVER 4 Mar 1854 in Mount Vernon; children: Nora, b. Jan 1857 and Clay, b. 1863/64. Respond to Alice Plane, 508 Oriole Drive, Evansville, IN 47715.

21 June 1992: John (Jack) H. OSBORN was superintendent of Evansville Cotton Mill from 1884 to 1908, died 1912. What became of family: Charles, b. 1853 at Cannelton, moved to Chandler, IN; Alexander, b. 1874, moved to Indianapolis; John Wm. OSBORN, b. 1878; Chas. Arthur OSBORN, b. 1900. Contact Karin M. Kirsch, 6007 Hogue Rd., Evansville, IN 47712.

5 July 1992: Seek information about the descendants of Charles (Carl) LINDENSCHMIDT, born 1828 in Germany, emigrated to Evansville prior to 1849; married Catherine. Known children: Charles, Henry, August, Joseph, Mary, William. Respond to JoAnn Miller, Route 3, 55 Quail Creek, Oxford, Miss. 38655.

27 Sept 1992: Seeking information or descendants of Sarah Olive (Balding) PURCELL, born Richland Co., Illinois about 1857; living Evansville in June 1926, wife of Claude PURCELL. Her parents were Jacob and Margaret (MORGAN) BALDING. Contact Pat Gaither, 402 New St., West Salem, IL 62476-1169.

25 Oct 1992: Hazel L. May Litherland requests information about the Evansville Cotton Mill and wonders if it was in operation in the 1864 era. Anyone who has any information should send it to her at 632 Ninth St, Tell City, IN 47586.

22 Nov 1992: Seek death date and place for Abraham WISE, living Union Co., Kentucky in 1900 with son Amos; probably died ca. 1903-1905. Son Charles WISE lived Evansville in 1910. Send information to Ann Wise McDaniel, Rt. 2, Box 191, Carthage, TX 75633.

28 Mar 1993: Wish to locate descendants of Charles FOREMAN (died Princeton, Ind, in 1917) and wife Lucinda BYRD who were married in Crawford Co., Indiana in 1893. Children were Harry, Carrie (may have married ---MASSEY) and Linwood FOREMAN. Contact John J. Quinkert, P.O.Box 205, Lanesville, IN 47136.

29 Aug 1993: John M. GEUPEL, born 1822 in Germany; died 12 Dec 1896; received citizenship in July 1855. Married Anna Elizabeth MANN and Hedwig E. SCHULTZ. Children: Charles, b. 1862; Louis, b. 1865; Lily, b. 1870; Theodore, b. 1874; Valeda, b. 1878. Family operated a business in the 400 block of Main St. in Evansville from 1855 into the 1900s. Write: Mrs. Bob Ervin, 328 Joyce St., Weatherford, TX 76086.

10 Oct 1993: Need information on parents of Margaret Holton LANDSDOWNE born about 1800 in Kentucky, who married Richard WESTROPE, (born about 1795) on 22 Apr 1813 in Knox Co., Ind. They were in Amite Co., Miss. later. Family tradition says that Margaret's father was killed in 1803 in Ky. and she and siblings Joel, Hilah and John were reared in Evansville by Mr. Evans, founder of Evansville Respond to Ms. Marlene Wilkinson, 1200 French Ave., Lakewood, OH 44107..

24 Oct 1993: Looking for ancestry and history of William Hunter MILEY, born 20 May 1869 in Indiana; ran away from home in 1883 to Newtonia, Mo. Married Sarah Alice DODGE 18 Dec 1890 in Joplin, Mo.; died 19 May 1937 at Pueblo, Colo. Send information to Arthur O. Miley, 5102 Longridge Ave., Sherman Oaks, CA, 91423-1514.

24 Oct 1993: Seek information on ancestors and descendants of James Wm. PECK (1837-1902) and Lucenda WOOLVERTON (1849-?). Respond to Lynne Walters Ooley, R.2, Box 408, Winslow, IN 47598.

21 Nov 1993: Seek information about descendants of James DAVIDSON (b. Ireland ca. 1827-28; died Evansville 22 Jan 1883) who married 1854 in Warren Co., KY to Ann RICHARDS (b. 1834 in Doddington, Cambridgeshire, Eng.; died 1919 in Evansville). Their children: Mary W. b. 1865 (?); Susie, b. 1858; William T., b. 1865; Hattie/Henrietta, b. 1869. Contact Betty Richards Kirkpatrick, 9901 Shady Pine Dr., Ocean Springs, MS 39564.

21 Nov 1993: Want information on Anderson WOODALL (b. GA 1839; died Pike Co., IN 6 Feb 1900); mar. Mary Ellen KINMAN (dau. of Henry KINMAN and Eliza HAYES) in Pike Co. in 1866. Had son James, b. ca. 1865. Want info. of any kind about James ASHBY who mar. Elizabeth COONROD 1836 in Knox Co., IN. Children: Daniel G., Benjamin F., John W., all born Knox Co. Daniel G. mar. Mary McCAIN in Pike Co., IN in 1864. Contact Mrs. Arlene Cato, R.R.1 Box 369E, Petersburg, IN 47567.

2 Jan 1994: Looking for death date and place of burial of Maria HINMAN STEVENS, born 2 Feb 1782 in Conn. or N.J., dau. of Asahel and Mary (HARRIS) HINMAN. She married 2) Richard STEVENS on 3 Aug 1805 in Ohio Co., KY. Lived in Warrick Co., IN. Children were James STEVENS and Serena/Edna who married Reuben J. BATES in Warrick Co. Send information to Wanda Galbreath, R.R.3, Box 143, Princeton, IN 47670.

2 Jan 1994: Seek information on Elizabeth BUECHLER, born 1834, died 1902, married Bernhardt VONDERSCHMIDT, lived in Jasper-St. Marks, Ind. area. Also wish info. about Agatha FETTER, born 1 Apr 1867, married Francis VONDERSCHMIDT (born 4 May 1858, died 1941 at St. Anthony, IN); and info about Elizabeth NEIMIER, born 1829, died 1913, married Balthaser BUECHLER, lived in Tell City, IN area. Send information to W.D. Franklin, Sweet William, 1521 Blueteal Dr., Brandon, FL 33511.

16 Jan 1994: Seeking information or descendants of Mayme CLAY HIGGINBOTHAM of Ingelfield, Vanderburgh Co., Indiana. Her father, William H. CLAY mar. 2) Lydia E. McKINNIS on 5 Feb 1885 in White Co., Illinois. Send information to Donna Moyer, Rt. #1, Box 13, Sims, IL 62886.

Note: Since these queries were published from 1991-1994 the people who requested information may no longer live at the address listed.

INDEX